The Story and History of an American Carnival

WOODEN HORSES AND IRON MEN

DALE W. MERRIAM, PhD, PE (ret)

authorHOUSE®

AuthorHouse™
1663 Liberty Drive
Bloomington, IN 47403
www.authorhouse.com
Phone: 1 (800) 839-8640

Published by AuthorHouse 02/22/2020

ISBN: 978-1-7283-4796-7 (sc)
ISBN: 978-1-7283-4797-4 (hc)
ISBN: 978-1-7283-4795-0 (e)

Library of Congress Control Number: 2020903693

Print information available on the last page.

Any people depicted in stock imagery provided by Getty Images are models, and such images are being used for illustrative purposes only. Certain stock imagery © Getty Images.

This book is printed on acid-free paper.

CONTENTS

FOREWORD

BY ALICIA MERRIAM

Dale would annually warn his drivers, especially the new ones, about the Pine Island Cheese Festival and the dangers lurking there...

He actually printed this on an official route slip that was handed out to all his drivers.

"Do not talk, flirt or otherwise fraternize with the Pine Island girls. I did it once and I've been doomed to a life of eternal bliss ever since"

Dale W. Merriam

Special thanks to:
Mary Alice Schulte Honz and Tom Merriam

PROLOGUE

It's my intention to write (and leave behind) my memories of an American carnival. It's a history of our carnival – a business that has been in our family for three generations – four if you count my grandfather's contribution, and that contribution was significant. I believe my story is typical of many, if not most, of the travelling carnival companies in the country. We're a small and tightly knit industry with about 400 identifiable and recognized "show "names nationwide. All travelling carnivals are as unique and individual as the men (and a few women) who own and operate them, but the similarities are huge. I believe that in telling the story of Merriam's Midway Shows I am also telling the story of a uniquely American industry. One that is colorful with its own lifestyle, its cast of characters, its sub-culture, and, yes, to some extent, its own language. Though this is not intended to be a scholarly work, considerable effort has been made to verify names, dates, locals and historic events, such as, the Columbian Exhibition of 1893 in Chicago – the acknowledged birthplace of the American travelling carnival. Having said the above I strongly adhere to the adage "When legend becomes fact, print the legend".

No names of individuals or names of places have been changed to protect the innocent (nor the guilty either, for that matter) – they have been too much fun to know not to receive full identifiable credit. Walter Lee (Shorty) Hall, Eugene Debs (Brownie) Brown, Walter (never had a nickname) Marston and Kokomo (never knew his real name) – you'll meet them all. The towns, fairs and celebrations (you will learn to call them "spots") visited ("played") also reflected middle-America and had their own quirks and personalities. Many of these were and are repeat dates of thirty and more years. For example we have been in Tama, Iowa every May since 1953.

Do not expect an expose' of the carnival business telling of crooked games, bawdy girl shows, and sneaking out of town one step ahead of the sheriff. In Chapter VI we'll talk about games, so watch for a couple of classic, funny carnival game stories. As far as girl shows, they simply don't exist anymore. As much as the Ferris wheel itself, they came out of the 1893 Columbian Exhibition along with the word "bally". I'm glad I was there to see at least the end of that era, and I can still hear in my mind's ear the call of the talker (not a 'barker') cry, "They shake it to the east and they shake it to the west, but it's on the inside where they shake it the best – come on down." You'll meet Gene and Katherine Woods, Chief Little Wolf and Dirty Gerty. Chapter III ends fittingly in Columbus, Nebraska, with a huge windstorm that blew down two Ferris wheels and a drive-in movie screen that was showing "Gone With The Wind".

The reader should keep in mind that we are a carnival and not a circus. Both carnivals and circuses travel from town to town and both sell cotton candy, but there the similarities pretty much end. The defining difference between the two is that you watch a circus to get enjoyment, but to enjoy a carnival you have to participate. You have to ride the Ferris wheel, throw the dart at a balloon to win a prize and walk through the mirror maze, bumping your nose as you go, to experience the fun. The laughter and thrills of a circus can be televised and beamed via satellite to your family room; not so with a carnival ride. To enjoy a tilt-a-whirl you have to buy a ticket, get on the ride along with twenty or so other screaming and laughing riders, and have your body slung around and around while you hope you don't lose your pocket change, your grip on the handle bars and the two corn dogs and the sno-cone you ate just before the ride. Another difference between the two is their origin. Circuses can trace their beginnings back to the old world. The Roman Coliseum was a circus experience. The lions ate Christians instead of jumping through hoops, but it was an animal act that the audience sat and watched. In medieval times there were court jesters and jugglers performing for kings, dukes and a few of their close friends. Carnivals, on the other hand, are a twentieth century American phenomenon. This will be talked about in Chapter I with an acknowledgement to the French who set the bar high - about a thousand feet high as a matter of fact.

This will be the story of a carnival and the people who lived and worked to make it operate for three quarters of a century. I know it's a story from my perspective, but that is the only perspective I have. I also know from experiences shared with other carnival owners over the past fifty-plus years, I'm not alone in my feelings and memories. Several years back, at the Nebraska Fair Managers Association meeting Jim Roller, the owner of Hale's Shows of Tomorrow, told me, In his opinion, "Owning and operating a carnival is the biggest boost the male ego can possibly have." Another friend of mine in the business, Bill Dillard (now deceased) who owned the Bill Dillard Exposition out of Texas, once told me, "Running a carnival is the last true and absolute dictatorship on the face of the earth". I've also been told, at various times, I am a dreamer and fanaticize about the way I wish things were. I hope that makes me a showman, because if I could choose any title for myself that would be the one. There is no way I could be considered a great showman, but I knew some and knew of others. And that is close enough for me.

As the story unfolds the reader will be gradually introduced to some of the expressions, style and slang used on the American carnival. When the slang becomes familiar it adds a precision to the language that is necessary to properly tell the story. When the men (and a few women) who run the rides are called "rideboys", the title is purposely written as one word as is the more familiar occupational title – cowboy. The single word, rideboy, will not be found in the Oxford English Dictionary as will the word cowboy. As will be explained in Chapter V, the only reason cowboys get more respect is that they had better writers.

I hope you enjoy the story as much as I have enjoyed living it. Let's begin.

CHAPTER I

THE BEGINNING –
THE EIFFEL TOWER AND
FERRIS' BIG WHEEL

The traveling carnival as we know it today and in this country is truly an American institution born and bred. It is as American as the cowboy and the prairies of the western states. It is an industry and life style that deserves yarns, songs, legends and heroes to tell its story alongside of Americans like Buffalo Bill Cody, Paul Bunyon, Pecos Bill, the Cardiff Giant and P. T. Barnum. If in the telling of these stories facts and legends intertwine, so be it. Conceived at a fair, inspired by engineering and industry, sustained by agriculture, the American carnival grew as America itself, grew. It prospered or withered in a climate of free enterprise, capitalism and more than just a little unabashed showmanship.

All things have beginnings, and more than a few have unintended consequences. In the late nineteenth century Paris was the acknowledged center of the western world for art, music, new wave thinking and industry. In 1889 all of these things were celebrated and showcased to the world through a gigantic fair – the Paris Universal Exposition. During the planning stages of that world's fair a tower was proposed – taller than any stone monolith possible – that would be a fitting monument to commemorate the French Revolution. With some hesitation at the beginning, Gustave Eiffel – known as "The Wizard of Iron" - and his engineering firm became interested in the project. An experienced bridge designer, Eiffel had already completed the interior framework for the

French peoples' gift to the United States – the Statue of Liberty – and made considerable contributions to the completion of the Suez Canal. The tower was to be made of riveted wrought iron and, at a height of almost one thousand feet, would be taller than any famous monument of the time.

When it was completed on March 31, 1889, for all its magnificence, the tower was not universally accepted. Critics thought it not in "good taste", it was gaudy and not in keeping with French art and history. Expectations were that it would be torn down at the conclusion of the Exposition. Like a carnival, perhaps it didn't appeal to the "upper crust society", but over two million fairgoers loved it. By the end of the fair the tower had recovered its 7.5 million franc construction cost and turned a profit. Eiffel's tower not only became a permanent fixture but the defining symbol of Paris thereafter. Eiffel's genius had set the bar for the planning of the 1893 Columbian Exposition to take place in Chicago celebrating the four-hundredth anniversary of Columbus's landing in America. By the time architect Daniel H. Burnham (along with his partner John W. Root) was appointed to head up the design and construction of the Chicago fair it was clear that Eiffel's Paris tower was the symbol to beat. The Columbian Exposition must be the best and have the best. Second place would not do. One newspaper reporter of the time said it simply, "America's pride was at stake".

As design and construction of the fair progressed, new and unique ideas for a unifying symbol were not forthcoming. Taller and more bizarre towers were proposed. There was talk of a tower that would pivot on its base. All were deficient in design and originality. Then, in 1891 Burnham was asked to address a banquet attended by a number of engineers and fellow architects. At that banquet was a young bridge engineer by the name of George Washington Gale Ferris, Jr. who listened intently as Burnham lamented about his problem. With the seed planted in his mind, young Ferris would relate later that the complete idea came to him on a Saturday afternoon in a Chicago chop house over dinner. Another example of the genius often released by a hastily sketched idea upon a napkin. In his own words Ferris describes the event. "...... It was at one of those dinners down at a Chicago chop house that I hit on the idea. I remember remarking that I would build a wheel, a monster. I got some paper and began sketching it out. I fixed the size, determined the construction, the number of cars we would run, the number of people it would hold, what we would charge, the plan of stopping six times in the first revolution and loading, and then making a complete turn, - in short, before dinner was over I had sketched out almost the entire detail, and my plan has never varied an item from that day. The wheel stands in the Plaisance at this moment as it stood before me then." Move over France here comes America at her best!

A quote of Daniel Burnham's was, "Make no little plans. They have no magic to stir men's blood". Certainly Ferris made no "little plans". His wheel was colossal. Not only was the scope of the project gigantic, but time was short with the scheduled fair opening of May 1, 1893 rapidly approaching. The fair didn't grant Ferris the concession to build his wheel until December 16, 1892 leaving only months to order materials, design and build – not to mention raise the estimated $350,000 cost. Components and material arrived in March requiring 150 railroad cars for shipment. The main axle – the largest steel shaft ever forged up to that time – weighed 45 tons and was 45 feet in length and 32 inches in diameter. The wheel itself was essentially a giant bicycle wheel 250 feet in diameter. Duke University professor, Henry Petroski's book Remaking the World describes eighteen engineering efforts that significantly changed the world. Ferris rates a whole chapter while Eiffel must share space in Ferris's and others. Petroski relates many of the facts pertaining to the enormous size of the wheel. Each of the 36 cars was the size of a trolley carrying 60 people each – 40 seated on swivel stools and 20 standing. Each car carried its own conductor to answer passenger's questions and/or calm any fears they may have. With 36 cars the total capacity of the ride was 2160. As many as 38,000 fairgoers rode the wheel in a single day – the price of a ticket – 50 cents.

The first car was hung on its babbitted bearings on June 10th. The grand opening was set for June 21, 1893 – a month and 21 days after the opening of the fair. The opening ceremony included Ferris, his wife Margaret, local dignitaries and several speeches with Ferris speaking last. He thanked and praised his wife, the fair and fair officials for their help and encouragement and concluded by dedicating his work to the "engineers of America". At the end of his remarks, Ferris was handed a golden whistle by his wife, Margaret, which he blew as a signal to start the wheel. As the great wheel began to turn the Iowa State band, attending the fair from

Ames, Iowa, struck up "America" and the Columbian Exposition of 1983 had its defining symbol.

Along with Ferris' Wheel, two other notable attractions at the fair would have a big influence on the soon to evolve carnival Industry. One was not really a part of the fair proper. Buffalo Bill's wild west show was set up outside the fairgrounds and could be attended without actually attending the fair. The show, grandly named Buffalo Bill's Wild West and Congress of Rough Riders of the World, was extremely popular and profitable. When the first carnival association – The Showmen's League of America – was organized in 1913 William F. Cody became its first president. The other profitable and popular attraction(s) on the Midway Plaisance (the concession and amusement area of the fair) was the Middle Eastern belly dancers. There were several dancing shows on the midway, and they all did a variation of what was to be referred to as "that dance" or "the dance". Contrary to belief after the fair, the exhibit called "Little Egypt" was not on the midway. This did not, however, stop girl shows both at the fair and those that traveled afterwards from referring to themselves as "Little Egypt".

Two new words came out of the Columbian Exhibition, and became additions to the growing carnival lexicon. These were "midway" and "bally". Midway, of course, came from the Midway Plaisance entertainment area at the fair. The word midway soon became universally accepted as the entertainment and concession area of a fair – the carnival. The other word, bally, was a new descriptive word that sprung from events at the fair. The Oxford American English Dictionary acknowledges its origin as turn of the century American. There are two stories about the word's origin, and it's possible that both might be valid. With the number of Middle East belly dancer shows on the Midway competing for customers, talkers (Notice that the word here is "talker" and not "barker". Barker is not a term used by outdoor, travelling showmen.) would cry out in loud voices to call potential customers into their shows. A popular phrase among the Middle East showmen was, "B'Allal Hoo", roughly meaning, "Thou Art God". Another phrase, "Dehalla Hoon", was used to call out the performers for a free, preview show on a raised platform outside the front entrance of the show. To the Western ear these phrases sound like "ballyhoo" which was soon shortened to its contraction, "bally". Now we have a new word. A word which was not needed before carnival type shows, but now it was. Bally, used as a verb, means to call in customers. When it is used as a noun it could mean either the short, free show in front of the entrance intended to give customers a sample of what to expect on the inside, or it could mean the raised platform upon which that free show takes place. Often this raised platform had an apron like canvas covering the front and two ends for appearance sake. This piece of the show tent naturally was named "the bally cloth", and along with pieces like the top, the sidewall, quarter poles it, also, was a specific name for a specific piece of equipment.

By October the great fair was over. Ferris' wheel had operated flawlessly for nineteen weeks, earned enough to pay its expenses including the construction cost, and return a cash profit to Ferris of $78,294.40. The gross sales were $726,805,50 at fifty cents a ticket. The fair received $211,805.00 which was 50% of the sales after the cost of the ride itself. Plans to move the ride to New York were discussed but ruled out when the moving costs were estimated at $150,000. In the spring of 1894 the wheel was disassembled and loaded onto railroad cars. The massive axel with hubs attached weighed over 70 tons and required a special car which had been designed to carry a giant Krupp cannon. In the spring of 1895 it was reassembled at a small amusement park in Chicago but could not attract enough customers to be profitable. It was to be moved one more time to St. Louis for the 1904 Louisiana Purchase Exposition. After the St. Louis fair the ride was never used again. The towers were dynamited, and the usable iron salvaged. In Indiana, about forty-five miles south of Chicago, a bridge across the Kanakee River was constructed from sections of Ferris' great wheel. George Washington Gale Ferris, Jr. died in 1896 of tuberculosis at the age of 38.

As the Chicago fair neared its closing date more and more discussion took place among the independent showmen and venders both on the Midway Plaisance and off the grounds in the area around Cody's wild west show. There had been a semi-official meeting on the grounds shortly after the fair started about how to increase attendance and other matters. The informal discussions and exchanging of ideas was a natural extension of that meeting. The idea of organizing into small groups and promoting "street fairs" at various cities and towns around the country soon developed. One of the first such organizers was not a showman at all but a scenic theatrical artist by the name of Otto Schmidt. Schmidt obtained financing and in the summer of 1894 fielded two units playing St. Louis, New Orleans, Toledo and dates in Texas. The first season was a disaster financially, but Schmidt was not to be stopped. With a spirit that was to become typical of outdoor showmen everywhere, he borrowed more money and framed the Chicago Midway Plaisance Amusement Company in 1895. The show travelled on a train of seven flatcars, six boxcars and enough coaches for 540 people. Their opening date was the New York State Fair in Syracuse. Now that's show business, and the tone was established for the coming century.

These early carnivals mainly consisted of shows and exhibits. Some of the first riding devices at those early fairs were crude merry-go-rounds. They were big, hard to move and powered by steam or were horse-drawn. The Kansas based Parker Company's merry-go-round with jumping horses and easier portability soon became popular with travelling shows. The Parker horses were carved with front legs extended to the front and the rear legs to the rear. The advantages of this particular frozen-in-action pose were several. It was a pleasing, uniform look on the ride. It was a compact shape with minimum vertical distance and, thus, took up less space in the transporting vehicle. And, last, the extended legs made convenient hand holds for two men to lift and carry the horse during set up and tear down.

The Ferris wheel, or rather the lack of, problem was also soon to be solved. The solution would come, fittingly, from a fellow bridge builder who had visited the great fair from down state Illinois. The Eli Bridge Company relates their founder's story on their web site as follows:

"In 1893 E. E Sullivan visited the Columbian Exposition, where he marveled at the original Ferris Wheel. Like George Washington Gale Ferris, Mr. Sullivan owned a bridge building business – Eli Bridge Company. As he took his first ride on Mr. Ferris' Wheel, little did he know that his life was about to change forever.

Despite skepticism from his family and the business community, Sullivan remained fascinated by the Wheel and was determined to build one of his own. He later collaborated with machinist James H. Clements and together they began construction of their Wheel on March 23, 1900. This first "Big Eli" Wheel debuted in Jacksonville, Illinois' own Central Park on May 23, 1900. The Wheel was a great success and in 1906, Sullivan incorporated the Eli Bridge Company by taking in capital investors to mass produce his wheels."

The Big Eli wheels quickly became the ride of choice for travelling carnivals. In 1919 the company erected a new building for manufacturing, and that building is producing wheels, as well as other rides to this day.

Another popular ride was the Whip manufactured by the W. E. Mangles Company and introduced in the mid-teens of the 1900's. The Tilt-A-Whirl, manufactured in Faribault, Minnesota by the Sellner Manufacturing Company, was introduced in the twenties and was an instant hit. With three or four of these rides a carnival was a "big carnival", and could play almost any fair in the country. McKennon's research indicates the first organized carnival to play an agricultural fair was Gaskill Carnival Company at the Minnesota State Fair of 1904.

If the birth of the American carnival industry can be pegged at the beginning of the nineteenth century, its childhood and adolescence probably lasted until the thirties. By the post-war years young adulthood had been achieved and the outdoor raveling amusement business was ready to prosper and get on with its life's work. Traditions, superstitions, slang, and even a language of sorts soon developed. Among one of the strongest traditions was, perhaps borrowed from agriculture – an industry to which carnival people have a great kinship. That is the tradition of the business staying in the family. Carnival ownership is often handed down from father to son. Most young men entering the business were born in the business. If you were not born into the business, a close option was to marry the boss's daughter. A young man or woman could walk on the lot and with a little effort become a rideboy, a ticket seller, or an agent, but to become a carnival owner is another matter. It's like becoming a farmer, if you had not had some early connection – like being the owner's son – you probably would not think to become a carnival owner. There are notable exceptions to be sure, but for the most part every important carnival today is in its second, third and even fourth generation of ownership.

As with most other industries, carnival people developed their own slang. Slang words are much more precise than trying to choose one or more of the 600,000 words in the English language to accurately define an object or event. The events or fairs at which a carnival sets up are "spots". You don't work at a spot, you "play" a spot. The game and food concessions are "joints". The actual area at the spot where the carnival sets up is the "lot". A "jump" is the move to next spot, either by rail or highway. A short jump is obviously fewer miles than a long jump, and a "circus jump" requires tearing down right after closing in one spot, making the jump and opening the following day in the next spot. And, the people who work on the carnival are "carnies". Carnies are very jealous of their slang, and do not like to be called "a carny" by anyone other than another carny.

But slang wasn't enough. As they traveled from town to town and from fair to fair they never stayed long enough to fit in socially with the existing community. Some fairs lasted a week, some a few days, and, as we will see later, maybe only one night. If they couldn't blend in and mingle with the local community their own mobile society was created to fill the void. This creating of a community of carnies eventually led to the development of their own language (of a sorts). If you were really "with it" – with the show, that is – you had better know how to speak "carny".

Carny, the language, is really a variation of pig Latin, and has been called "Z-Latin" by some sources. Pig Latin was developed in England as a secret language and formed by transferring the initial consonant or consonant cluster to end of the word and adding a vocalic syllable, such as an "a" sound. Thus, pig would become ig-pay. To speak carny you would keep the syllable order but insert an "ea" sound in middle of the word and add a "z". the word pig become pee-a-zig. A full sentence might be, Key-a-zen yee-a-zoo tee-a-zawk key-a-zarny? The answer would be either, "Yee-a-zess", or "Nee-a-zo", or a blank look – depending if you were "with it" or not.

With their own language, their own lexicon of words and terms – some, such as "bally, belonging to no other industry –and their unique beginning, travelling carnivals brought a new and exciting form of entertainment to early twentieth century America. By the twenties the carnival industry was well established serving fairs, festivals, celebrations and privately promoted (still dates) nation-wide. Mostly travelling by rail and featuring more shows and exhibits than rides, the early carnivals were soon providing midway entertainment at fairs and festivals from border to border and coast to coast. Carnivals, like the family farm, became family enterprises where the wives and children could work along side the men for the betterment of the enterprise. Sure, the carnival boss – the image of the show – was usually the patron of the family, but behind that façade was often as not a good strong woman (and, if he was lucky, a smart daughter and a couple of good strong sons helped as well).

Many of these early carnivals being organized would last decades into the new American century. The seeds of one of these had been already planted in the rich, black soil of central Iowa.

The other new addition was a fourteen seat, gasoline powered kiddie train purchased by Wilbur. Manufactured by The Miniature Train Company of Rensselaer, Indiana, it was a real classic, and much sought after by collectors today. It was a carefully detailed model of the streamliners of the post-war era right down to the head light on the locomotive, the hand rails by the doors and the windows down the sides of the cars. The train consisted of the locomotive and three open top passenger cars. One car had four seats, three forward facing and one rear facing. The second car and the end car had five seats each, four forward facing and one rear facing. The track could be set up in various configurations but generally as an oval approximately twenty feet by forty feet. The purchase price was thirty-two hundred dollars – a big price for Wilbur who was used to building his own. The train was powered by a four and one half horsepower, one cylinder, air cooled Wisconsin gasoline engine. The "engineer" sat in an open topped compartment at the rear of the locomotive much like the fourteen passengers behind him.

The routine was, wait until all the passengers were seated – if an adult were not excessively big they could ride with their child -, collect a ticket from each passenger, start the engine, give two or three soundings of the electric horn, advance the throttle and circle the oval track four or five times. There was no fence around the track to prevent people from walking across the path of the train so the engineer had to be ready to stop or slow the train if someone or something got into the pathway. What kept small children from walking in front of a moving train? – their mothers. Dale was the first engineer that season and for the next five seasons to come. Around and around the track he went under the watchful eye of his grandfather. For this he was paid seven dollars a week for the first two seasons, twelve dollars a week for the next two and twenty dollars after that. For that salary, Dale, also helped set up and teardown the train and kiddie cars. When Wilbur died in July of 1954 he left the train to Dale in his will. The next year the train was sold and the money used to purchase U.S. Savings Bonds for Dale's future college. The train, as it turns out was the first of two really dumb things Dale sold. The second was to be a "57 Chevrolet convertible which was a gift from his father on his 18th birthday. Both of these machines went on to become classic collector's items, and their values today would be very similar.

By spring the new show was ready. All the trucks were brightly painted red with Merriam & Robinson Shows on the sides of the trucks and trailers. Each truck door was emblazoned with its identifying number painted in fancy scrolled font covering the entire door. Trucks carried numbers like 42, 27, and 38 even though there were probably less than a dozen in the entire fleet. Bob Robinson, along with his bingo and other games added a monkey side show featuring a couple of trained chimpanzees one of which would participate in a banana eating contest against a local boy drawn from the crowd gathered in front of the show. Robinson also purchased an army surplus carbon arc search light and mounted it on a flat bed semi trailer. This was located in the center of the midway and lighted up the sky with a circling beam that could be seen from miles away. Gene and Catherin Woods from Rathbun, Iowa booked their girl show at many of the spots to round out the back-end. Al and Bob attended the state fair association meetings in Iowa, Minnesota and Nebraska and the 1947 route was booked.

In 1947 the ride list was:

> Ferris Wheel
> Merry-go-round
> Chair-O-Plane
> Loop-O-Plane
> Tilt-A-Whirl
> Kiddie Cars
> Miniature Train

Each ride had its own ticket box (booth) with the exception that the Kiddie Cars and Train shared a box with Myrtle doing the selling, Wilbur running the Cars and Dale as the Train engineer. The Tilt-A-Whirl and Loop-O-Plane were twenty-five cents On Kids Days matinees all rides were ten cents. Al was always proud that he never ran a ride for a nickel. Another factor in the ticket prices was the federal excise tax. In those days and until the first year of the Eisenhower administration there was a 20% tax on amusement ride tickets. A twenty cent ticket returned only $0.167 to the ride owner. State sales tax (if any) had to be paid on top of the federal. Tickets less than a dime were exempt from the 20 % tax. Since the Iowa sales tax was included in the 10 cent tickets the actual price of admission was less than a dime. At the time Minnesota had no sales tax so the 10 cent tickets were worth a dime and the 20% tax was due. For those reason dime matinees in Minnesota featured nine cent tickets. And Edna did it all without computers and electric calculators.

During these early years, with the war just over, tools and materials, with which to build and repair were often scarce and expensive. Power tools were especially not available in a small mid-western town such as Ogden. Early on Al realized he needed a power hacksaw if he was to get any serious work done on the rides and the trucks that transported them. No tool of that type and size was readily available. He could buy steel locally and parts like, pulleys, belts and an electric motor. What was the Merriam solution to a problem like that? Al hand sawed the frame sections to size, fashioned a vise for holding the work to be cut, and after about a week he had a working power hacksaw that would cut three-inch channel with surprising ease. The finished machine was about four feet in length, two feet in height, painted bright orange and was used every year in winter-quarters well into the eighties

Over the winter Al made another big improvement in the show by purchasing a new two-abreast Merry-Go-Round from the Allan-Herschell Company of North Tonawanda, New York. This ride was stunningly beautiful with modern florescent lighting, chrome platform and horse rods and twenty brightly painted "half-and-half" horses. They would be dubbed "half-and-half" by later collectors in that the bodies were carved from wood while the heads, necks, legs, and tails were of cast aluminum. The horse shoes were of a separate casting and attached to the hooves with screws. To pull the semi-trailer that would haul the new ride Al bought a new 1948 Ford truck which he outfitted as a semi-tractor with a fifth-wheel and vacuum brakes. In February of 1948 Al and his friend Clem Smith of Stratford, Iowa made the trip from Ogden North Tonawanda in the new gray, Ford and semi-trailer to retrieve the ride. When they arrived at the factory the ride was set up, in all its shiny glory, for inspection and then disassembled and loaded in the semi trailer Al provided. The two young Iowa men took advantage of where they were to visit Niagara Falls before returning to Ogden. This Merry-Go-Round, serial number H8747 is currently registered as an historical ride with the National Carousel Association, and, like the Tilt-A-Whirl purchased the year before, is still in use on the show. The serial number was stamped on an oval, brass name plate attached to the front of the "organ" (the sound system cabinet). When Dale assumed ownership of the show in 1974, Al removed the name plate from this, somewhat, vulnerable place and presented it to son, Dale, in a simple ceremony on the midway one day before opening. The cost of the ride in 1948 was approximately $10,000.

Clem Smith with partner, Ben Mesenbrink, owned the Boone Valley Shows from nearby Boone, Iowa (eight miles from Ogden and the county seat of the same county). McKennon lists that show operating from 1948 to 1953. Clem lost his arm in an accident setting up a Ferris wheel in 1953, but remained active in the industry as a booking agent for other big carnivals including Bob Hammond Shows and the Bill Hames Shows, both out of Texas.

Carnival owners have a strong individualistic tendency and the desire to "go it alone". If it is true that, being a carnival boss if the greatest boost the male ego can possibly have, it is probably also true that the "boost" is best enjoyed solo. For this reason and probably some others the two partners, Merriam and Robinson, decided to part ways after the 1948 season. Bob Robinson framed (the word "framed" was/ is used to mean organize or make ready) his own show – Robinson's Greater Shows and toured into the mid-fifties. Al Merriam, a few years younger than his partner and with the support of a good wife and family, introduced to the industry for the 1949 season, Merriam's Midway Shows.

The winter of 1948 – 49 was a busy one for Al. All of the trucks were repainted to display the new show name. The color theme was red trucks with black fenders, and the talents of a local Ogden sign painter were put to much use. Marlin Balcer worked at the municipal power company in Ogden and painted in his off hours. Over the years Marlin and Al became close friends, and the painter's work was evident on the show for the next fifteen years. Another new ride was added for the coming season – an Oct-O-Pus manufactured by The Eyerly Aircraft Company of Salem, Oregon. This popular, higher capacity ride replaced the Loop-O-Plane and the Chair-O-Plane as the show started to take on a new look. As new games and food concessions were booked for the coming season, new people and personalities came with them. A significant newcomer was the new bingo operator from Gulfport, Mississippi, Ken Davis and his wife Eleanor. Ken and Eleanor previously did a "high pole" acrobatic act with Ken doing one-armed hand stands high above the crowd, and Eleanor swinging from a trapeze. It was obvious that the act was Ken's love and not his wife's, and they were now in the game business. Still, Ken might be seen walking down the midway on his hands just to show he hadn't lost his touch. The had one son, Wayne, who was about two or three years younger than Dale. Wayne tragically died at about age twelve in a boating mishap off-shore in the Gulf near their home.

The Davis bingo was unique in that it was self-contained on a semi trailer and not under a canvas top as were all bingos in the past. The sides and ends of the trailer opened upward to form awnings that shaded and protected the counters and players. Seats were placed on two sides and the end of the trailer. The trailer itself consisted of shelves displaying the prizes to be won. With modern fluorescent lighting and polished stainless steel paneling the effect was pretty spectacular for the time. The most unique thing, however, was the Hammond electric organ mounted in the front of the trailer. Not only was Ken an acrobat but also a gifted organist. Each night, before a large enough crowd had arrived to start the games of bingo, Ken would play about a thirty minute concert of familiar tunes on the organ. At the close of the evening's play, again, he would entertain the midway with a brief concert.

Some of the dates on that first 1949 season were Gowrie, Iowa over July Fourth, Boone, Iowa, Kossuth County Fair in Algona, Iowa, Rice County Fair in Faribault, Minnesota and Steamboat Days in Winona, Minnesota and the Platte County Fair in Columbus, Nebraska.

Preparation for the 1950 season was a busy one with Al and Edna attending fair meetings in Des Moines, Lincoln, St. Paul and Chicago at the Sherman House Hotel. The Iowa meeting held in Des Moines just before Christmas, 1949 was especially well attended by major carnivals of the day. News coverage in Billboard magazine mentions Sunset Amusement Company, Al Martin's 20th Century Shows (a name that is still in operation in the 21st century) Boone Valley Shows and others, including, of course Merriam's Midway Shows. Also mentioned as an attendee was Iowa Attorney General Robert L. Larson of Johnson County. A meeting was reported to have been held between the AG, several carnival owners and some fairs. The subjects discussed at that meeting were not revealed, but is was well known that Larson intended to strictly enforce the state's gambling laws. Any game charging to play and awarding a prize based on a chance outcome was gambling. Bingo was gambling, picking up a lucky duck from a tank of water was gambling, throwing a baseball at a beer bottle was gambling – it was all gambling. By a coming twist of fate, Attorney General Larson was to have a lasting impact on the Merriam family, but in a wonderful and unexpected way.

When the show went on the road for the 1950 season there were two significant changes. One was the addition of the Cannon Valley Fair in Cannon Falls, Minnesota to the route. Cannon Falls replaced Gowrie, Iowa as the 4th of July spot. Their dates were July 2 – 3 – 4, sometimes beginning on the first, but always ending on the 4th. The fair remained on the Merriam route for next sixty years. The second addition was the Cundiff family who had the cookhouse. Red and Florence of Hollywood, Florida had three children, Carrie, a year younger than Dale, Edna, a year older and their brother, Howard, the same age as Dale's sister, Margret. Howard's nickname was Slugger. He was known only as Slugger. His parents called him Slugger, his sisters called him Slugger, for all practical purposes, his name was Slugger. The Cundiffs and their cookhouse and hired man, Whitey, stayed with the show until 1960. As will be seen the fifties were a great decade to be a teenager, and being a teenager on Merriam's was the greatest of all.

Over the winter Grandpa Wilbur (Web) carved eight smaller horses and built a kiddie horse and buggy ride – a pony cart ride – to add to his kiddie cars and little train.

In 1950 the ride list was:

> Ferris Wheel
> Merry-go-Round
> Oct-O-Pus
> Tilt-A-Whirl
> Kiddie Cars
> Miniature Train
> Pony Cart

The Cundiff cookhouse changed the social structure of the show in a very positive way. They served three meals a day from before seven in the morning until about six-thirty at night when the evening midway business startd to pick up. It was a social gathering place for ride help, jointees, and all show personnel to have coffee, eat and share conversation. A blackboard carried and special instructions for the day, such as, "Open tomorrow 1:00 P.M." or "Midway trash must be picked up before closing". Coffee was a nickel in a heavy mug with a handle, Coke in a bottle was a dime, and a T-bone steak dinner was a dollar (with coffee). Meal tickets were available for $5 and carried a $5.50 value. Most of the ride boys bought meal tickets, and the $5 would be billed directly to the office to be deducted from their weekly pay. The 4th of July always featured fried chicken. Red Cundiff was the cook working out of a kitchen built inside a converted school bus while his wife, Florence, and Whitey waited on the counters on the three sides of the framed tent that abutted the kitchen. Red and Whitey opened the cookhouse before seven for the breakfast crowd, and Florence would come to work mid to late morning. About 6:30 in the evening Red would take a quart of milk and six-pack of beer and go to the trailer leaving Florence and Whitey to the night time grab joint business. Whitey, by this time, has worked both shifts. One advantage was that he had a short commute as he lived in the cookhouse once it closed and he had dropped the awnings.

For the evening business the presentation changed into what is called a "grab joint" – midway fast food. The featured item was footlong hot dogs served from a steamer and topped with chili. The price of this delicacy in 1950 – 25 cents. Whitey would stand behind the center counter hour after hour with his bally, "Get 'em while they're hot. A loaf of bread, a pound of meat, and all the chili you can eat".

Some of those years Cundiffs would come to Ogden a full month or more before the show opened and feed the crew in winter quarters who were painting and getting the show ready for the coming season. All three of the Cundiff children finished several school years in the Ogden schools with Dale and Margret.

In 1950 a set of interconnected, small events took place that would have a lasting and a wonderful effect on the Merriam family. They could not even suspect that Iowa Attorney General Larsen's crack down on carnival games would have such results.

As the 1950 season began it became ever more clear that with no games of either chance or skill being allowed, a carnival midway with only straight sales was not fun and not a real midway at all. Al looked north to neighboring Minnesota, and cancelled some of his Iowa spots. Two game owners, Russell Frey and Chuck Rudisill went on a booking trip to find Minnesota dates for late June and early and July. They had pretty good luck, and one of the new dates was Plainview, Minnesota (on highway 247 and about 25 to 30 miles from Pine Island. The wheel foreman that season was Eugene Debs, "Brownie" Brown. The show arrived in Plainview, Brownie checked into the local hotel. (In the 50's most small towns had a hotel. The rooms were 3 or 4 dollars with a bath down the hall.) Sometime that day a man drove up in an out of state car and ask to see the boss. Finding Al he explained he owned the carnival that was currently in Pine Island for their Cheese Festival, and he had a help problem. He had no wheel man and no one capable of setting up his wheel. Could he borrow our wheel man and pay him to set up his ride.

It was kind of an unusual request, but Al said it was okay with him if Brownie wanted to make a few extra bucks. Dale was sent to the hotel to get Brownie, and the deal was made. Al was smart enough not to send Brownie alone. Help stealing was a regular, intra-industry crime, and they just might not send Brownie back. With that Al, Brownie. Chuck Rudisill and young Dale piled into Al's 1947 Mercury and headed for Pine Island. Upon arrival, the four found a celebration in full swing with a crowd waiting to be carnival customers, and a carnival not quite set up and ready. Brownie found his ride and crew, and went right to work. While the wheel was being set up Al and Chuck had some work to do also. Somehow, and without causing too much of a stir, they found out quite a bit about the Cheese Festival. Chuck Rudisill located a few of the committee in charge of the celebration and invited them for a soft drink at the Rainbow Café and to meet the owner of a different carnival – one that can be set up on time. In a few minutes more than four hours the wheel was up and carrying people, Brownie had been offered a job (which he turned down) and Al had a contract for the midway at the 1951 Cheese Festival. Stealing spots was also an intra-industry crime regularly perpetrated.

Another significant event that marked the 1950 season – the second season - for Merriam's Midway Shows was the playing of the Cannon Valley Fair in Cannon Falls, Minnesota. The dates of the fair were July 2 – 3 – 4 and replaced Gowrie, Iowa as the shows fourth of July spot. Under Al Merriam's ownership the show only played two "fourth spots" – Gowrie and Cannon Falls. The fair became a longtime favorite of the Merriam family. Speaking one time to the local Rotary in later years, Al, making reference to Guy Lombardo and New Years Eve, said, "when I go I'm taking the Cannon Valley Fair with me." He didn't, of course, neither did Lombardo, but a long term relationship existed between that fair and the Merriam's Shows for many years and into the 21st Century.

The next three seasons, 1951, 1952 and 1953, proved to be growing years for the fledgling carnival. The ride arsenal was increased by the addition of a used Spitfire purchased from the Sunset Amusement Company, a carnival based in Excelsior Springs, Missouri, and a Pony Cart Ride made by Wilbur Merriam. The principal concession owners (and children) were Ken and Eleanor Davis (Wayne) of Gulfport, MS – Derby and Bingo, Red and Florence Cundiff (Edna, Carrie, Slugger) of Hollywood, FL – cookhouse, Russell Frey of West Union, IA – role down, Woody Gathier of Iowa Falls, IA – scissors buckets, Otis and Vi Porterfield (Larry, Kenney) of Kansas City, MO– glass pitch (Otis was also employed as the show electrician), Bill and Eilene Talley (Pete, Julie) of Long Beach, CA – cotton candy, Roy and Lilia Nigg of Des Moines, IA – shooting gallery, Roy Drier – root beer and novelties and Chuck Rudisill – dart game. Gene and Catherine Woods of Rathbun, IA played a few dates with their girl show (Catherine was the "girl" – Gene was the "talker"). Gene's father also traveled with his own show, and would play an occasional date with Merriam's. The father's name was Iron Wood (note the lack of an "s" on the end of Wood), and his nickname was (Are you ready for this?) Rusty.

The early fifties were good times for most Americans and those in the carnival business were no exceptions. Fuel was cheap, help was plentiful, and the mood of the country was upbeat and ready for fairs, festivals and celebrations. Except for that pesky Attorney General Larson in Iowa, and the 20 per cent tax on tickets, government regulations and restrictions were relatively few. With a little innovation, even AG Larson's ban on games of chance could be circumvented. Ken Davis made use of his electric organ in the front of the bingo trailer to change his corn game into a game of skill. The new game was called "Musical Knowledge". Davis had new cards printed, somewhat larger than the bingo cards, that had names of songs in the squares instead of numbers. These were old, standard songs like, "Old Black Joe", "My Darlin' Clementine", and "Row, Row, Row Your Boat". Davis would play a few bars of a song and if you recognized the tune and had it on your card you placed a kernel of corn in that square. Four kernels in a row or the four corners was a winner. The lucky winner would call out in a loud voice, "Musical Knowledge". You couldn't call out, "Bingo" because, of course, you weren't playing bingo. Bingo was illegal in Iowa, and maybe even the hollering the word out loud was a jailable offense. The game was no longer a game of chance because the outcome was determined by how skillful the individual players were at identifying the songs played. The concept for all its innovation was just a little silly. Although the game was determined to be legal in a few of the Iowa spots it was not profitable. The bingo playing public wanted their bingo – not some silly game where you had to listen to "Three Blind Mice" being played on a Hammond organ.

Ken Davis' other game was a really flashy, eighteen player Derby. It consisted of a back lighted, eighteen row board with figures of race horses at intervals across the board. Each row had the names of the Kentucky Derby winners for the past eighteen years. Each player would roll a wooden ball through his game box. The ball could go through a fast or slow chute and advance the player's horse accordingly as it was lighted on the big board. The game operator would call the race in his best track announcer voice, and award the winner prize coupons – one coupon for each player in that race. Coupons could be saved and redeemed for prizes any time during the event. Bigger prizes required more coupons. The game cost ten cents to play and was enormously popular with the midway customers. Unfortunately is was just as enormously unpopular with Iowa AG Larson. To counter this, Ken tried to run the game for a nickel as amusement only and offer no prizes. That didn't work either and the game soon went the way of Musical Knowledge. It was a better idea to, "point the trucks north".

At the close of the 1953 season Al became interested in venturing into the game part of the business. "Shots" Wallace of Fulton Missouri had booked a game with the Show in 1953, and it caught Al's attention. Now, with a nickname, "Shots" and, license plates on his car that read, "FUN" it was a safe bet that his specialty would lean toward shooting guns for entertainment. His game was called "Sky Fighters", and consisted of a trailer full of arcade type guns which offered 100 shots for five cents. No prizes were awarded – you shot for fun, excitement and a high score. Al tried to buy one of the units from "Shots", but no deal could be struck. At this point the only solution was the typical Merriam solution. Al decided to build his own.

The 1953 trade show and convention in Chicago afforded the opportunity to shop for and compare coin operated games of all kinds and among them were several that simulated shooting at airplanes. Al was most impressed with the Genco Company's Sky Invader game. The machine on display at the trade show was set to accept dimes and, for that ten cents the player got 300 shots at enemy airplanes as they flew past. The guns were big, flashy and had a lighted scoreboard that showed the shots taken and hits scored. No prizes were awarded, the game was amusement only and a typical game lasted about thirty seconds. The player would peer into a movable gun sight to see the black light, illuminated targets flying by and then try to align the gun sight with the moving airplane and press the trigger button. Al thought these guns had advantages over the ones "Shots" Wallace had. The Sky Invaders would be new and probably be less of a maintenance problem. A second advantage as they were a dime a play. Al never liked to sell anything for a nickel. Ten machines were ordered for delivery to Ogden Iowa – ASAP.

The Carnival business was and is a small industry. Most of the principal players and especially the carnival owners know each other. It wasn't long before his purchase was the "buzz" of the convention. Ten machines at $385 each, by most arithmetic, gets awfully close to four thousand dollars. A trailer still has to be built, bought or otherwise acquired, lighting purchased, and considerable work framing the final joint. In 1953 this was a sizable sum to invest in a game concession when a major ride sold for, perhaps, $12,500. Al came home to Ogden from the convention with a big winter's project ahead of him and just a little smug that he had caused somewhat of a stir at the convention. He also, unknown to him or anyone else, had forged one more link in a chain of events that would change the Merriam family and the history of the Show forever.

After the 1952 season the Merriam family moved into a much newer and more modern house in Ogden. The new house was four blocks east and closer to downtown and the schools. It was, however, still between US highway thirty (The Lincoln Highway) on the front and the Union Pacific double track railroad on the rear. An interesting bit of trivia about those tracks is that west bound trains run on the south tracks and the east bound trains run on the north tracks. Some claim that an English engineer laid out the tracks. Whatever the reason it makes these tracks unusual in this country. The Merriams were nicely settled in their new house by election day, 1952, allowing Al and Dale (now thirteen) to stay up quite late watching Eisenhower defeat Stevenson on television. As the hour grew later Edna (who was in bed) got up and said Dale should come to bed

"That young boy should go to bed, Al,"

"He's watching history being made, Edna. He'll never forget it."

And, he never did. Eisenhower won easily, putting the first Republican in the White House in twenty years. One of his minor campaign promises was to get rid of the 20% tax on amusement tickets. The Merriams "Liked Ike".

A major addition soon to be added to the new house was detached double garage with a concrete floor, natural gas heat and really good insulation. A local contractor did the work with instructions from Alva that if "he struck a match inside the garage on a cold winter day the temperature would go up at least two degrees". By the winter of 1953 – 54 – Dale's freshman year at Ogden High School – one bay of the garage was ready to receive the ten new Sky Invader machines. Dale's job was to try out each of the new guns – several times over – to be sure they worked okay. They did.

Before the building of the new concession trailer could begin in earnest the route for the 1954 season had to be finalized. The Iowa fair meeting in Des Moines was about the last piece of business to be conducted before the Christmas season. The Merriam tradition was that the family Christmas tree would be put up after Edna and Al came home from that convention. The Minnesota meeting was in mid-January with the Nebraska convention the following week at the Cornhusker Hotel in Lincoln. Often Al attended the Nebraska meeting alone. By this time Edna was about "conventioned out" as she put it.

To gain a little experience with the operation and maintenance of his new machines and to possibly gauge their popularity and player appeal, Al decided to try placing a few of the machines in restaurants and coffee shops in nearby towns. Taking Dale with him one afternoon Al quickly scouted out locations in local restaurants in nearby towns of Paton, Dana and the local truck stop – The Gunyon Supply Company – in Ogden. Al's good friend and Shrine brother, Jack Gunyon, was the owner. The guns proved reliable and popular, but after a couple of weeks the experiment was over and the task of building the concession trailer had to be taken on in earnest.

An already manufactured, 16 foot, flatbed, drop axel trailer was purchased and backed in to one of the bays of Al's garage. It was late January in Iowa, and the natural gas heated garage was put to good use. All ten gun cabinets were cut off so the gun would be at player-eye level with the machine sitting on the trailer deck. The scoreboards were brought forward for increased visibility, and the trailer sides were made to fold down to give the whole joint an open look. Marlin Balcer, who lived within walking distance, did the final signage. As a last minute addition, Al purchased two penny gum ball machines and fitted one on each side of the trailer between two of the gun cabinets. Dale got to keep all the profits from these two machines – first year profit was about thirty-five dollars.

By the first of May all winter quarters work was finished, the Sky Invaders were parked outside gleaming with a fresh green and yellow paint job, and the crew was ready for the first date of the 1954 season. That season was to be without Dale's grandfather, Wilbur as were all future seasons. When the show left winter quarters Web was in Mary Greeley Hospital in Ames, Iowa with a cancer type illness. He was later transferred to his home in Ogden and died that July while the show was playing a date in Buffalo, Minnesota. As fate might have it the next date on the route was the Merriams' home town of Ogden – a two day event called Fun Days. After teardown in Buffalo the family drove all night to arrive in Ogden. Enough time existed to make arrangements, set the show up, have a funeral with a reception in Myrtle's home, operate the carnival for the two days of the event, tear down and continue with the route. Wilbur's Miniature Train Ride – purchased new in 1947 – was still on the show but Dale was no longer the engineer. Dale now had his flashy, new Sky Invaders to manage. Ownership of the little train – the one he ran when he was eight years old - passed to Dale in Wilbur's will.

The Pine Island, Minnesota Cheese Festival – the one Al stole in 1951 – was still on the route in 1954, and one being looked forward to by Dale as a potential good spot for his Sky Invaders. Pine Island not only was and still is a good spot it is a delightful community. With a population of 1298 in the mid-fifties, it is located on US 52 eighteen miles north of Rochester and 70 miles south of Minneapolis in beautifully green and rolling southeastern Minnesota. The young men worked on the farms, played baseball during the summer and had no idea of the encroaching threat setting up carnival rides on their main street. The young women were blond, willowy and moved with the grace of goddesses. Their mothers (the Methodist women, the Catholic women and the Lutheran women) were the world's greatest cooks – no question. Their method of testing cream for proper richness was to pour the cream in an open bowl and stand a spoon upright in the center. If the spoon fell over the cream was not thick enough. A pint of this cream could be purchased from the local cheese factory for fifty cents. Alicia's Grandpa Charlie worked at the cheese factory, and her folk's dear friends, Wilbur and Tina Iwen owned the local Iwen Box Factory (and became quite wealthy).

The carnival was set up in about a two block area of Main Street between the store fronts. having just been re-done a year or two before, the street was smooth and wide with parallel parking along each curb and pull in center parking in the middle. The carnival had plenty of room to still allow the parade to go down the middle of the street. Some of the games that would usually occupy the center of the street did so. When the parade came the carnival workers simply picked up those games and move them out of the way. After the parade had passed they were moved back.

One of the businesses on Main Street was the Ahneman Beauty Shop. Hilda and Arnie were both hairdressers. They owned their building and lived in the apartment on the second level along with their sixteen year old daughter, Alicia. Dale's Sky Invaders were located in center of the street almost in front of the Ahneman shop. Another Cheese Festival tradition was to have high school girls walk through the crowd with baskets of cheese samples from the local cheese factory. Alicia was one of those "cheese girls" along with her friend and banker's daughter Barbara Stucky. As luck would have it (the same luck, perhaps, that caused AG Larson to direct Al Merriam toward Minnesota) the two girls thought that tall, lean boy running the Sky Invaders might like to taste some cheese. Well, the cheese was tasted, talk was talked and it became apparent there were one too many cheese girls. The girls thought they should get back to the crowd and their job of passing out cheese samples. What took place once they were out of sight of the Sky Invader operator has never been revealed. Did they toss a coin, did they draw straws, did they play paper, scissors, rocks they have never told. In any event, whatever casting of lots took place, Alicia came back to talk to that tall carny from Iowa and Barbara didn't. What might the outcome have been had the coin flipped the other way, who knows. Alicia and Dale celebrated their fiftieth wedding anniversary December 28, 2011.

One thing almost caused a problem. Larry and Kenny Porterfield (my two best friends on the show) and I were not always truthful when we talked to the town girls. We didn't have to be. We were going to be gone in a day or two and in a different county telling lies to another willowy blond whose mother was a great cook. When I was fifteen I thought I could pass for a year or two older than I was. If I told the local girls I was seventeen or eighteen the size of the field greatly increased. I was alright claiming to be eighteen until my mother made an appointment with Alicia's mother to have her hair done. In the course of clipping, curling and chatting the conversation got around to Dale and Alicia. Her mother innocently asked, "How old is Dale". Then my mother did the unthinkable. She told the truth! As she tried to explain to me later, "I couldn't say I didn't know!" Anyway, it all worked out. See closing paragraph above.

CHAPTER II

THE WHEEL YEARS –
A MAGICAL TIME NEVER
TO BE RECAPTURED

A t the dawn of the fifties the dependability and rider popularity of Big Eli wheels made it desirable for many shows to carry more than one wheel on their midway. Royal American Shows – the unchallenged gold standard of the time and for many decades into the future – had four Eli Wheels in their backend. With the four wheels lined up, side by side, and a huge lighted sign that read "ROYAL AMERICAN SHOWS", each word filling the three interior spaces between the wheels, it was nothing short of spectacular. The Sunset Amusement Company carried three wheels for a short time, and show owner, Ken Garman, claimed the flash of those three wheels allowed him to book the North Dakota State Fair. When Eli Bridge came out with a newly designed trailer mounted wheel that was much easier to move, Bernard Thomas of the Mighty Thomas Carnival bought a pair of them. One wheel just wasn't enough for the carnival who really wanted to compete for the bigger dates. One show owner, writing to the Eli Bridge Company, put it as follows, "One wheel – little show, two wheels – big show". With the sale of the Spitfire at the end of the 1953 season, Al made up his mind to add the second wheel.

The wheel presently on show was a No. 12 model, like the more popular No. 5, only bigger. A No. 12 was 45 feet high while a No. 5 was forty. The each had twelve seats, were set up and torn down in the same way, but the pieces were just a little bigger. The spokes were 2 feet longer, the top towers were 2 ½ feet longer, the A-frame or derrick for erecting and lowering the towers was bigger, and the block and tackle rigging required a triple block and a double block where as the No. 5 required only two doubles. In any event, only another No. 12 would do to match up with the one currently on the show. In the spring of 1954 Al found a No. 12 in a park in Baytown, Texas, near Houston. The deal was made and with the show up and operating at an early spring date in Boone, Iowa, Al and his good friend from Ogden, rural mail carrier, Loren Roe went for the newly acquired wheel.

When disassembled a ground model wheel (A ground model ride is one that is completely disassembled and loaded in a separate truck.) is a fairly compact load. A No. 12, properly stacked and racked will fit into a box 24 feet by 8 feet by 10 feet. In other words, it would fit in a 28 foot semi-trailer. It would be convenient if the trailer had a double deck so the seats could be placed on the top deck to keep them separate from the iron on the lower deck. One of the two trailers required to haul the Tilt-A-Whirl fit that description pretty well so Al and Loren were off to Baytown. They had six days to drive from Iowa to Texas, tear down the new wheel and return in time to unload the Tilt trailer and tear down the show in Boone. The truck tractor they drove was a red 1950 Ford that Al had purchased new from Moffitt Ford in Boone, and except for a small gas tank that required them to stop every eighty miles for fuel, the trip was uneventful. The ride had been sitting in an amusement park near the Gulf and as a result some rusting made teardown more difficult. The hubs were rusted to the axel so instead of removing them, the axel and hubs were loaded as a single unit. Ferris had the same problem when he moved his wheel in Chicago. Luckily, an Eli axel with hubs weighs, perhaps, 300 pounds. Ferris's weighed over 70 tons. Once back in Ogden, Uncle Snort's machine shop came to the rescue. Snort had a hydraulic horizontal press with a bed and stroke long enough to press the two stubborn hubs off the axel. Snort had designed and built the press himself. He was much like his brother, Web – if you needed something you made it. Snort was somewhat eccentric – he didn't like long hair on men, idle chit-chat or Democrats – but if you needed some machine work done, he was your man.

For the first couple of weeks that year the show was close enough to Ogden to allow some "winter quarters" work to be done to the new wheel.

It was immediately called "the Texas wheel" to differentiate it from the "old wheel". In about two weeks time, the Texas wheel had been painted, the LeRoi gasoline engine tuned up, and the hubs made so they would easily slide on and off the axel. In some ways the Texas wheel was in better condition than the old wheel, but for all practical purposes they were identical. Once loaded on its own semi- trailer, the Texas wheel was ready to be set up beside its twin, and together they added new flash and booking power to the show.

In 1954 Dale had just finished his freshman year at Ogden High School, and once on the road he had his Sky Invaders arcade concession to run, and three kiddie rides to set up and tear down. These jobs had to be done, but they had no power to hold his heart like those two wheels standing in the backend. Setting up and tearing down a ground model Big Eli Wheel had a rhythm and choreography to the process that would often draw a small crowd of fascinated onlookers. In a period of about four hours, beginning with a location stake marking the spot and a semi load of iron, a crew of four men could assemble a forty-five foot wheel, twelve seats and all, ready for fairgoing passengers. No small part of Dale's attraction to Ferris wheels (and especially Big Eli Wheels) was inherited from his father, Alva. But, neither was Alva alone in his attraction to the ride. Bernard Thomas, the late owner of The Mighty Thomas Carnival of Lennox, South Dakota and, later, Austin, Texas could fondly relate being the wheel foreman for his uncle and show founder, Art B. Thomas. As an example of just how fast he could move a wheel, Bernard would tell of the season they played 29 spots in the month of June. He claimed to have played two spots in one day – one in the afternoon, then tearing down, moving setting up and playing a few hours in the evening. Whether they tore down again that night doesn't matter. That's "moving pig-iron".

The first wheel foreman I remember on the show was "Brownie", but by the time the second wheel was added, Brownie – whose real name was Eugene Debs Brown, and Brownie was quick to point out he was named after Eugene Victor Debs, nineteenth century American socialist and five time candidate for the presidency of the United States – had been given the job of merry-go-round foreman. I have forgotten the name of the wheel foreman in 1954, but I distinctly remember some things about him. He was careful, methodical, but not very fast. He had "love" and "hate" tattooed on the tops of the fingers of his right and left hands, respectively. He had large strap hinges tattooed on the inside of his elbows so that the hinges would open and close as he would bend his elbows. Under each breast nipple were the words "sweet" and "sour", again right to left respectively. He was the first wheel foreman I worked with as I began to learn my craft.

With the beginning of the 1955 season Walter Lee "Shorty" Hall appeared on the scene with prior Ferris wheel experience. Shorty was, in fact, short – probably no more than 5 foot three or four at the most. That measurement would be about the same whether taken head to toe or shoulder to shoulder. Shorty had muscles, was fast and liked the ladies. It was Shorty and the other ride boys of that period who turned the setting up and tearing down rides into a competitive, athletic event with the wheels setting the standard in many cases. Dale worked with Shorty that summer during most of these "events" while running his Sky Invaders during operating hours. Dale was the "top" man, and Shorty "pulled the ropes". Four hours "up" and three hours "down" was an acceptable time. Three, and one- half hours up and two, and one- half hours down was competitive, while two and one half and two was in the championship range. Whether Dale and Shorty were champions or not was never recorded, but in their prime they would have accepted the challenge.

There are four distinct stages in setting up a ground model, Big Eli Wheel - four quarters in the event.

Stage one involves leveling and setting the bottom towers. This can be accomplished by two men if for some reason the full complement of four was not available. The base piece is first unloaded, placed in position, blocked and leveled. Once this has been done the location of the wheel has been established. The bottom tower sections are stood upright by hand, the necessary bracing is attached with steel pins, and the towers are blocked and leveled front to rear. None of these parts are numbered or coded for assembly. The various sections either fit one way only or are interchangeable. As much as possible all the parts come out of the truck in the order they go on the ride so as to avoid double handling as much as possible, The top towers, especially No. 12 top towers, are longer and heavier than the bottom towers and are definitely a three man lift. The task is to attach the axel and hubs to what will be the very top and to stand them (the top towers) directly on top of the now vertical bottom towers. In this stage the top towers are assembled horizontally on ground level ramps to be hoisted vertical in stage two. The gasoline engine that will drive the wheel is put into position along with the clutch and brake mechanism and the big "bull gear" that supplies power to the cable drive. On the inboard side of this bullgear is a spindle or windlass to be used with the rope block and tackle when the heavy hoisting begins. With a typical four man crew the foreman has done the leveling, they have worked together unloading the various parts, the second man and two helpers have assembled the top towers, and the foreman has made ready the motor and drive mechanism. The time expired so far would be about 60 minutes.

Stage two is going to be raising and leveling the top towers. This stage would not take as long but the effort would get a little more intense so now was the time to take a brief break, "smoke 'em if you got 'em" and maybe send one of the town kids watching the set up for a bottle of pop. The first step was pull the top towers up the ramps and knee bracing with the triple/double rope and pulley so that the bottom of the top towers could be pinned to the top of the bottom towers. The towers now formed two side-by-side right triangles with the ground and the bottom towers forming the right angle and the top towers completing the triangle. Now a simple derrick, called an "A frame", could be assembled and with the double pulley block and tackle and two or three wraps of the rope around the bullgear spindle the foreman could pull the towers upright while the second man and the most able of the two helpers pinned them in place. Once they were vertical the towers would be leveled left to right and secured with the proper guy cables and steel bracing. The structure now stood some twenty five feet tall and was ready to receive the twelve spokes that would form the wheel. The time expired for stage two would be about 45 minutes, including the cigarette break. A later foreman, Hubert Herren, cut some time from the set up by reducing the smoking time. He had a curious way of sticking the butt end of a lit cigarette to one of his upper front teeth during almost the entire set up. He could laugh, cuss, give directions, and spit while all the time crouched over the bullgear pulling ropes and not disturb his smoke. That cigarette was stuck as if with Gorilla Glue.

Stage three was, by far, the most fun, required the most teamwork, and usually attracted an audience. This is when the twelve spokes were attached along with the rim irons, and the wheel begins to resemble a wheel. Now a four man crew is required. Each of those four men (Sorry, ladies, but it was men's work. Merriam's had one great lady wheel man, Marion Nealon, but that was in the nineties and a different type of wheel.) had a specific title and job to do in the choreograph. The foreman was going to "pull the ropes', assemble the rim irons on the clutch side (the left side) and direct all activities. The second man was going to "work the top", assemble the off side (the right side) and make sure the spoke tailers assembled the spoke correctly. The spoke tailers were usually of little or no experience, since they were to do a task requiring about six simple operations and then repeat the task twelve times they could learn the job fairly quickly. After about three or four spokes they got about as good at the job as they were going to get.

The assembled spoke consisted of two sides connected by angle iron spreader bars and two cross cables to be used for truing the spokes when the wheel was completed. The spoke, lying almost horizontal on two inclined wooden planks, was hoisted up to the hubs at the top of the towers by means of single rope and pulley attached to the top end of the spoke assembly. The foreman would take a couple of wraps around the turning bullgear spindle, and by keeping the rope taut by pulling, the gasoline engine would supply power to hoist the spoke. The top man had to climb the lattice-like structure of the tower and be ready to guide spoke ends into the slots of the awaiting hubs. When one side had been pinned he would step across on a spreader bar to pin the other side. The spoke tailers held the "tail" ends – one on each side – off the ground and helped guide the spoke as it was hoisted into its place in the wheel. To assist the top man in inserting the pins into the holes in the hubs the spoke tailers would move their ends of the spokes up and down in about a six inch arc at the top man's command. Now, the spoken instructions from the top man was not, "Please move your end in a 6 inch arc". The command was, "SHAKE IT!", and if workers from three or four rides away couldn't hear what was intended only for the spoke tailers, well, then the top man simply wasn't playing his role.

With the first spoke pinned the top man would reach out, grab the rear right guy cable running from the top of the tower to the end of the base below and simply slide down. It was the quick and easy way down and only required pair of leather gloves. No sense taking the stairs when a down elevator is available.

I tried it once in the rain not thinking about how slippery a wet cable might be. I hit the ground in a heap, slightly dazed and with a chipped elbow. After that I walked up and down if it was raining. There is a scene in the Elvis Presley movie, "Roustabout" where he is running the wheel and flirting with the boss's daughter. When the foreman comes on the scene, Elvis, wanting to look busy, quickly grabs a rag and begins to rub the guy cable and says, "Just greasing up the wheel cables". Now, the guy cables would never get grease applied, and, when I first saw the movie, I hoped the top man didn't try to slide the cable during teardown. I still get a twinge in my right elbow when I see that particular movie scene.

With the first spoke in place the tailers assemble the next set, the wheel is repositioned, rim irons attached and up the tower the top man goes to repeat the cycle eleven more times. The time to attach one spoke was about 3 to 5 minutes. The time for completion of the "spoking" would be about 45 minutes to one hour. It was not at all unusual for the whole process to be completed with the only words spoken by anyone were the top man's, "SHAKE IT!"

With the pinning of the twelfth spoke and the last rim iron the circle is complete and the ride is beginning to be recognizable as a Ferris wheel. The assembly time so far has been about two and a half to three hours depending on the breaks taken, how hot it was, and, perhaps, how much rest the crew got the night before. Anyway, stage four was going to take about forty-five minutes, and it was another "smoke 'em if you got 'em" moment.

At this point the completed wheel was free- wheeling and could easily be turned by hand. So that all the spokes (and later the seats) would run uniformly and evenly spaced between the towers the wheel had to be trued. This was accomplished by a pattern of adjustable cables running between the spokes and a set of cross cables on each set of spokes from the end near the axe to the outer end near where the seats will be. The spoke cables were adjusted first with the foreman doing the measuring from the tower to the spoke, and the second man standing in the center of the wheel doing the adjusting with instructions from the foreman. Usually two complete revolutions were necessary to get the precision required. Next, the foreman and the second man "walked" the rim irons and adjusted spoke to spoke to achieve parallelism between the spokes. If the spokes were not parallel the seats would not hang straight on the ride. The decorative lighting could be attached at this time, as well. The spoke tailers are kept busy carrying parts from the truck, handing them to the foreman and second man and picking up extra blocking, etc. around the ride. The foreman has coiled the ropes and put away the block and tackle in the proper box himself. The level, also, goes in the rope box. Nobody touches the ropes but the foreman. He would have given you a cigarette, maybe shared his women or whiskey, but don't touch his ropes.

Now with the lights and cables in place the drive cable can be looped over one of the cable drive blocks (called "elephant ears") and by rotating the wheel threaded through each elephant ear so that it completely encircles the wheel. With the cable in place and properly tightened two things remained in order to have a completed wheel. The twelve seats have to be hung and the ticket box had to be set up. In the 1950's each ride had its own ticket box and it was carried on the same load. The price of a Ferris wheel ticket was 25 cents.

The seats were carried on the top deck of the open rack trailer. This kept them out of the way of the rest of the ride during set up, and made for easy access when they were to be installed on the wheel. The foreman simply backed the truck up close to the front of the wheel, and the seats could be hung by two men directly from the truck. The wheel could now be turned (under power) to the next position, the seat hung and so forth. In order to keep the wheel in reasonable balance, seat one was hung first, then 7 aned 8, then 2 and 3, then 9 and 10 and so on until all twelve were hung.

The time for this stage 45 minutes to an hour. The total time required for the completion of the set up would be in the range of 3 ½ to 4 hours depending on the heat index, availability of cold water and cigarettes, and the quality of the spoke tailers. It was hard, thankless, physical work, and really great fun.

Wilbur and Myrtle didn't come out for the 1954 season. Wilbur was sick with what turned out to be cancer and was bedridden when the show left winter quarters. Dale looked after the three kiddie rides – the Miniature train, pony carts and little cars – and ran his Sky Invaders.

The years from the 1955 season through the 1962 season were very stable, consistent and productive years for the show. Otis Porterfield was the electrician and had the glass pitch and bingo. Larry and Kenny were Dale's best teenaged friends along with Edna and Carrie Cundiff and Butch Butler from Austin, Minnesota. Butch moved to California with his parents in the early sixties and went on to own one of the largest and most successful carnivals in the country. Russell Frey had the roll down, and later on expanded a little bit with a nickel roll and actually invented the Crazy Ball joint on the show.

Several rides were traded and added during these eight seasons that gave the show a facelift and a bigger look. A ground model Miler kiddie coaster was purchased from an amusement park in Marion, Iowa. Wilbur's kiddie cars and pony cart rides were sold and replaced with a new King car ride and a second King ride without any vehicles. The original ponies and carts were retained and used on the new King ride. A couple seasons later two more new King kiddie rides were purchased: an electric train and a flat airplane ride. Dale's train was sold and the money put in US Savings bonds for Dale's future. The final addition was a new King Frolic ride. By the beginning of the 1960 season the ride list was:

1. Merry-go-round
2. Two Ferris Wheels
3. Tilt-a-whirl
4. Oct-o-pus
5. Frolic
6. Coaster
7. Kiddie cars
8. Pony carts
9. Train
10. Airplanes

The show was lean, organized and had a crew that could move it with a minimum of lost time and motions. Of course, they would get drunk, wander off, get married, have grandmothers die or just blow for no reason at all, but when they were there they worked and knew their jobs. They could drive the trucks, fix a broken light, maintain the gasoline engines that powered the rides, and keep a supply of grease rags on hand procured from the local town kids in exchange for a free ride or two. If a ride foreman happened to be the one who fell by the wayside, for some reason, the second man was often capable and ready to be promoted and take over. As often as not this was a chance for the newly promoted rideboy to show what he could do. This was not unlike a football player who has been riding the bench all season and gets to take over the quarterback position and a chance to win the big game. In anticipation of teardown, even rideboy's outfits were important. It was not un usual to buy new gloves a couple of days ahead just to be ready. Boots were polished, and sweatshirts and jackets selected and hung in the truck at the ready. The wheel foreman and secondman had their ballpeen hammers hanging in the wheel towers in exactly the proper position. The signal was the merry-go-round music. When it stopped on teardown night the show was officially closed. At that point each crew member was expected to know exactly what piece they would reach for first to start the teardown. In the case of the merry-go-round Bobby Arbuckle would first cover the organ. (The "organ" on the Allan-Herschell merry-go-round was in fact a sound system that played 45 RPM records. When it was new in 1948 it came with a record changer that played 78 RPM records that contained "live" band organ music recorded at the factory. The evolution was from 78 RPM records to 45 RPM to endless 16 mm tape to 8-track tape to cassettes to cd's to a solid state chip.) Bobby would have the canvas cover draped over the top of the organ in horizontal pleats such that with a simple flick of his right wrist the canvas cover would flutter down over the awaiting organ as if it had a life of its own. The first task of tearing down the merry-go-round was completed. Elapsed time: seconds.

Dale had his Sky Invaders through the 1957 season, and was responsible for the Miler coaster and the Frolic. The wheel foreman during the first couple of years was Walter Lee (Shorty) Hall. Shorty would come and go more than once during that period. The closing foreman was Hubert Heeren who had learned his trade working with Shorty (and Dale). While Bobby Arbuckle was flicking his right wrist Hubert would have super glued a cigarette to one of his upper front teeth and had started to fold toe boards on the wheel seats. Dale was responsible for the Miler coaster and the Frolic. There wasn't much doubling up on the rides in those days. Most rides had their own crew so that all rides could be worked on at the same time. The coaster and Frolic, for some reason were exceptions. For one reason, they were fairly quick to tear down with most of the tasks being of the tote and carry variety. Dale and two "green help" would be the crew, and could complete each ride in about an hour. Of course Dale would rather have been in the back end working on one of the wheels. If he really hustled he could, often as not, get his two rides down and make it in time to work the top on the second wheel.

Two memorable wheel events —one teardown and one set-up - come to mind during that period. One was in Willmar, Minnesota at the annual Kaffe Fest. The show was set up down town on the streets around the Kandiyohi County courthouse. The streets were not wide enough to set the two wheels side by side so they were located side by side, all right, but facing the courthouse one block apart. For whatever reason(s) we had a six man crew — two top men, two men who could pull ropes (Shorty and myself) and two spoke tailers. Remember it takes four men to take out the spokes but some of the tasks, such as resetting the wheel and loading the spokes in the truck can be accomplished with two men. Dale and Shorty's solution was simple enough. Take the spokes out of both wheels at the same time and make the spoke tailers run back and forth between the two wheels, up and down the alley. After all, it was only a block, and the office was paying these guys a dollar an hour.

The second memory occurred in Pine Island. Shorty was not with the show that particular season, and I do not remember who the foreman or the second man were. I must not have worked with them much that year to made a lasting impression. We would get the streets about seven in the morning and open that evening at six. I was certainly hoping for an easy set up. I had other things on my mind than setting up carnival rides, on the other hand, I know first things came first. What I didn't know was that during the night the wheel foreman blew and took the second man with him. This left no experienced people at all to set up the two wheels. I didn't know how my Dad was going to cope as I followed him around laying out the lot. One compromise would be to set up only one wheel. I should have anticipated his solution. As we walked up Main Street toward the bank corner he casually picked up two pieces of two-by-four blocking and continued to the end of the street. Placing the two blocks, one on each side of the street, to indicate the center and angle of the two wheels, without looking up said, "Set one wheel here and one there". No higher compliment could a father pay to a son. I didn't quite make opening with the second wheel, but they were both open at closing time. An interesting post script is that somehow my father knew where Shorty was, called him and flew him into Minneapolis in time for teardown.

The 1956 route card lists thirty-three spots between the May 9th opening in Albia, Iowa and the September 24th closing in Greenfield, Iowa. Eight of the jumps that year were "circus" or "over night" jumps. One of the spots was a one day event in Titonka, Iowa followed by an overnight jump to the Kossuth County Fair in Algona, Iowa. One of Al's strong points in booking a route was in finding or developing first of the week spots. Most fairs and celebrations wanted to have their events over the weekend. The trick was to find an event that would run Monday and Tuesday thus allowing the previous event to end on Saturday and move on Sunday, or if the previous event ended on a Sunday it could be followed by one that ran Tuesday and Wednesday. Al was good at it and left behind a long list of first of the week spots. Some of these are still on the route today. In 1956 some of the dates that filled that bill were: Fredericksburg, Iowa, Lakefield, Minnesota, Mountain Lake, Minnesota, Grand Meadow, Minnesota, Titonka, Iowa and Curtis, Nebraska.

Dale graduated from Ogden High School in 1957 – at the greatest time in American history to be a teenager. Teenagers had their own music, their own dress, bright futures ahead of them, drove the greatest cars ever built in Detroit and three days out of the summer the show would be in Pine Island. Alicia had graduated in '56 and was attending Macalester College in St. Paul. Dale's high school graduation gift from his father was a new 1957 Chevrolet convertible (aqua marine in color) which, properly equipped with a trailer hitch pulled the Sky Invaders. Carrie Cundiff, now seventeen, was the driver and followed what ever ride truck Dale drove. Most of the time that year Dale drove the coaster truck - a 1954 chevrolet straight truck with a gas engine and a 5-and-2 transmission. It was a sixteen foot double deck open rack with the top deck extending over the cab. Eight pieces of track plus the train of five cars went on the top deck. The remaining track, jack stands, fence, loading station, and the chain sections went down below. That fall Dale enrolled in engineering at Iowa State College (soon to be University), Ames, Iowa.

The seasons of 1958, 1959, and 1960 were a period of relative stability on the show. Al was plaged With the coming of the 1961 season changes for the show were coming – both those apparent and those not so apparent. Dale would be graduating from Iowa State at the end of the first summer session which seemed to require a decision about what to do next. In 1961, if you were male, non-student and single with no dependants there was some threat of being drafted. The call of the carnival business was still pretty strong and overshadowed any desire to work in industry. With two years of basic ROTC at Iowa State Dale applied for Air Force Officer Candidate School but failed to pass the physical. The show was in Denison, Iowa that spring while Dale was at Offutt Air Force base in Omaha making application. When he arrived back at the show with the disappointing news Al was ready with "plan B". This suggestion could have only come from that father directed to that son under those circumstances. Al said, "Why don't you call Jack Eyerly in the morning and buy a trailer mounted Loop?"

This idea wasn't entirely off the wall. They had talked about it before, but now it, all of a sudden' made sense. The Eyerly Aircraft Company was a popular and very active manufacturer of amusement rides located in Salem, Oregon. The Oct-O-Pus was purchased new from them in 1949, and the company president, Jack Eyerly, and Al had become good friends. Their new product, the trailer mounted Loop-O-Plane, was similar to the one the show had years ago except it had two passenger cars instead of one, thus doubling the rider capacity, and it folded up for transport on its own semi-trailer. It would be the first such trailer mounted ride on the show. Al had looked at the ride the previous November at the Chicago trade show. It would be new, flashy and a nice addition to the show. The questions were: is this something Dale wanted to do and would one be available for the 1961 season. Of course Dale wanted to do it, and a morning phone call revealed that one could be available the last week in June. The selling price was $13,500 which made it the highest priced ride on the show at that time.

The show had a spare GMC, gas, single axel tractor which Al agreed to loan to Dale for the 1961 season. Loren Roe, Al's mail carrier friend and fellow Shriner would drive to Oregon and deliver the ride to Cannon Falls, Minnesota for the July 2-3-4 Cannon Valley Fair. Dale was still finishing his last summer session at Iowa State but met Loren in Ogden so he could travel with the ride to Cannon Falls. Loren drove the entire way until they got just outside the south gate by the fairgrounds. There he stopped and changed seats with Dale so the proud new owner could drive his flashy new ride right on location that the equally proud Al had marked with a lot stake. Everyone on the show came to look at and admire this new ride. It was amazing how it all folded up, it was ablaze with multi-colored fluorescent lights, the hydraulic cylinder did most of the heavy lifting, and even the ticket box folded together in one piece.

Al, Loren and Dale proceeded to have the time of their lives setting up the new ride for the first time. Obviously the biggest toy any of the three of them had ever played with. And then a snag was noticed. The rest of the crew had gone back to their own rides to continue the set up. For some reason the Miler coaster crew was having trouble. They couldn't get the track level. They couldn't position the truck just right to unload the train. They just needed advice and help. Al turned to Dale and said, "Go over and help that coaster crew. Loren and I can finish up your Loop." Like the wheels in Pine Island a few years earlier, it wasn't long before the coaster up and ready. At 35 cents a ticket (all other rides were 20 and 25 cents) the new Loop-O-Plane grossed more than the two wheels on July 4th. Dale ran his own Loop-O-Plane and drove the truck for the remainder of the 1961 season. He paid the office for the salary of one ticket seller plus ten percent of the gross sales as a privilege (the nut) for booking the ride on the show. This ten per cent was in addition to the fee paid to the fair or committee and whatever sales tax was due.

As the fair season just got underway in Minnesota – the end of July – it was learned that this would be the last season for the Sunset Amusement Company of Excelsior Springs, Missouri. This well known carnival was owned by Al and Edna's good friends, Ken and Florence Garman. Al had bought the Spitfire from them in 1951. They had operated a very successful carnival and were at the age that they simply wanted to retire. Without a buyer on the horizon to take over the entire business the second option was to sell the rides and other equipment piece meal and walk away from the route. Two of the early fairs on the route were the Fayette County Fair in West Union, Iowa and the Olmsted County Fair in Rochester, Minnesota. Al had played the West Union Fair in 1959 and 1960 before losing it to Garman. It's hard for non-show owners (and, also, show owners wives) to understand that there is booking and there is friendship and one has very little to do with the other. In a small and cliquish industry like the carnival business it is quite possible to be fierce competitors and remain good friends. This was the relationship between Al and Ken Garman.

In addition to the upper-midwest fairs, Garman had a good route in southern Missouri and Arkansas including Labor Day and five weeks following. Merriams were closing the week after Labor Day in Nebraska. All of this scenario coupled with the fact that Merriams now had a new, flashy Loop-O-Plane and a son ready to try his wings offered some new opportunities. It is not know who called who (Al or Ken) but a deal was made that Dale would bring his Loop and two King kiddie rides in to the Olmsted County Fair in Rochester and then again toward the end of the route to play Bethany, MO, Slater, Mo, Lamar, MO, Dexter, MO, Harrisburg, AR and Caruthersville, MO. Dale was to leave his own show after the Platte County Fair in Columbus, NE and meet Sunset in Bethany with the Loop, Coaster and two King kiddie rides (Cars and Pony Carts). After Merriams closed the week after Labor Day brought the Tilt to Dexter so Dale had one more ride for the last three spots.

Rochester was great fun. It gave me a chance to be out on my own, and experience life on another show. Some things were different and some things were much the same. Each ride had it own ticket box and you turned in your ticket numbers and paid the office each night. I don't know what the percentage but probably between thirty-five and forty percent. We must have had to supply our own ticket sellers because Alicia drove back and forth from Pine Island (18 miles) and sold tickets. I must have hired a seller for the other two rides. I lived in a motel just outside the fairgrounds and drove the Loop tractor back and forth. Bill Stablefeldt, an old rideboy and his wife lived in Rochester and worked on the kiddie rides. After Rochester I joined our show in Algona, Iowa at the Kossuth County Fair. Alicia, who graduated from Macalester College the year before was getting ready to drive (a 1958, turquoise and white Chevrolet convertible) back to Southern California for her second year of teaching kindergarten in Garden Grove.

After Rochester and by the time they got to this southern route Sunset had sold several of their rides. The bumper cars and the Eyerly Rock-O-Plane were sold and left after Rochester. An interesting insight to the industry as it was in 1961 is that it was not unusual for the foreman to go to work for the new owner of the ride. This was the case of Garman's Rock-O-Plane foreman. He had worked for the previous owner and when

Garman sold the ride the foreman considered himself sold along with it. When Ken Garman sold his Scrambler ride at the end of the 1961 season, again, the ride foreman went with the new ride and worked for the new owner. During the off season, Al bought a new Scrambler for the next year and hired Garman's Scrambler second man to be the new Merriam foreman.

The first spot for Dale on the southern route was the Harrison County Fair in Bethany, Missouri. It was a tight jump from Columbus, Nebraska to this northwest Missouri fair ending on Labor Day. Dale lived in the Loop tractor, learned the rules of the new show, and settled up with the office every night after closing. One of the important things to learn early on was how to get along with the concession manager, McManus. This was a position that didn't exist on the Merriam's Shows. "Mac" was like an assistant manager and took care of details that Ken Garman delegated or didn't care to deal with personally. Mac was Garman's son-of-a-bitch. As it turned out Mac and Dale hit it off very well and right from the start.

The next spot was Slater, Missouri – a town of about two-thousand – located about eighty miles east of Kansas City. Though geographically still in the northern half of Missouri, in 1961 Slater was ideologically as far south as Dale had ever been. He was soon to learn this the afternoon they were setting up. This was a street celebration, like Pine Island, and the midway was up and down Main Street. It was a hot, Indian summer day, and Dale, his coaster man and local black teenager Dale had hired were setting up the coaster. At one point they decided to take a pop break in the nearby, local restaurant. Dale said he would treat, and the three of them sat at the counter to place their order. The waitress brought the pop, set two down on the counter and quietly but firmly told the black teenager that he knew better than to sit at the counter. He had to go to the kitchen to drink his pop. After the break the three of them went back to work, side by side, carrying coaster track and assembling the ride.

After Slater it was south on US71 to Lamar, Missouri, the birthplace of U.S. President Harry S Truman, and another street celebration. The jump from Lamar to Dexter, Missouri was a little more exciting. Having only operated his carnival in Iowa, Minnesota and Nebraska, Al had failed to buy the necessary Missouri truck licenses. Also, the Interstate Commerce Commission was just beginning to get involved with truck safety and regulation. Driver's log books were a new thing requiring drivers to record things like hours driving, total hours of service and fuel stops. There was a great deal for Dale to learn and that September of 1961 the institution of higher learning was a Missouri Highway Patrol Weigh Station on US60 near Houston, Texas County, Missouri. When all three of his trucks got stopped at that scale Dale was told he could go no further until he saw the judge in the morning about not having the proper Missouri licenses. Just then concession manager McManus drove up to the scale house door in his Cadillac. Never one to be intimidated by lawmen, Mac burst through the door pulling a wad of bills, roughly the size of a cantaloupe, from his front pants pocket. Dale will ever remember his words and his entrance as he said – while dropping two or three one-hundred dollar bills on the floor just to get everyone's attention – "What do you need, Dale, a thousand or two to get loose?" The end result was, with Mac patching the deal, no money was required, Dale continued on to Dexter with the promise to come back during the week and pay a small fine, and Al would purchase the proper licensing in Columbia. It was obvious that there were things for young Dale to learn beyond his education at Iowa State.

Having closed the weekend after Labor Day, Al brought the Tilt south for the next two spots. The Poinsett County Fair in Harrisburg, Arkansas followed Dexter and then Caruthersville, Missouri for the final spot ever played by the Sunset Amusement Company. After getting the trucks back to winter quarters in Ogden, Dale moved back into his old room in the house with Al and Edna and began to think about his future. Another educational moment for Dale could be summed up with a well know carny saying, "No spots, no money and November". A quick glance at the calendar revealed it was, indeed, a long time until spring. Perhaps a quick glance upward would have revealed the stars were aligning themselves such that significant and permanent changes were coming for Dale, a certain Minnesota girl teaching in California, and the show itself.

Shortly after getting the show put away Dale went with Al on a booking trip to Missouri and Arkansas to re-sign Harrisburg and Dexter and make a few new contacts for 1962 and future years. That trip gave Dale a first hand look at the way old time carnival booking was conducted. First phone calls (some times it was a letter or a telegram) were made to the fair of interest to determine when the fair's board of directors could meet with the interested carnival. If more than one carnival was interested – and this was usually the case - the any and all competitors would be invited to the same meeting. Each carnival would be represented by the owner or, as was often the case in those days, a general agent or booking agent. At the appropriate time each carnival's representative would be invited into the Board Room and make his presentation while the competition waited their turn in the outside ante room. If a decision was to be made that night all waited in the ante room while the board compared notes, discussed, voted and arrived at their decision. During this decision process the competing agents – who all knew each other - smoked, talked about the good and bad of the past season, the up-coming fair meetings, and where they were going next. If a decision was made that night the winner was called back into the board meeting to sign the contract and the losers would snuff out their cigarettes and drive into the cold to their next stop.

Upon returning from that trip Dale began working on two rather significant plans. One was one of the dumbest ideas he ever had and the other, undoubtedly, the best he had ever done or could ever do his entire life. The first was to trade cars. Why would anyone want to trade off a low mileage, great condition,1957 Chevrolet convertible that you owned free and clear? Ignorance is no excuse. Anyone with half a brain would have know that this was going to become a classic car of all time – an icon for the decade of the fifties. Any way the trade was made and Dale was driving a new, white 1962 Impala hardtop with red interior. Alicia was beginning her second year of teaching kindergarten in Garden Grove, California, and living in a house on Balboa Island with three other girls – all teachers. This was the good life – single, carefree, southern California, nineteen-sixty-one and driving a 1958 Chevy, light blue, convertible.

A steady stream of letters, each carrying a 6 cent U.S. air mail stamp, was keeping that chance meeting over a sample of cheese in 1954 alive. One of the letters from Alicia carried the news that she was coming home to Pine Island to attend the wedding of a friend, Karen Franzmyer in Hastings, Minnesota. Would Dale like to attend and visit a day or two in Pine Island? The next several event seemed to take place with blinding speed, and since this is the story of a carnival and not a romance novel the details can be summarized fairly quickly. The wedding in Hastings was held. A proposal of marriage was made and accepted. Plans were made with typical efficiency by Alicia and her mother, Hilda. Alicia returned to California an engaged women (with the promise that a ring would be forth coming). Alicia and Dale were married in the Glass Chapel, Portuguese Bend, California on December 28, 1961.

Upon arriving in California Dale searched the want ads in the Los Angeles Times for his first engineering job. With the ink barely dry on his degree in Industrial Engineering from Iowa State and no real work experience he thought getting a job was simply a matter of picking two or three from the companies advertising for engineers and scheduling interviews. In 1961 he was exactly correct. Within a week of arriving in California Dale was working as customer service engineer for Kaynar Manufacturing Company in Pico Rivera - making fasteners for the aircraft industry. Alicia continued teaching kindergarten in Garden Grove. The newly-weds both knew, however, Dale's dream was not making lock-nuts and selling them to Boeing. He had a new Loop-O-Plane to operate, and he had to follow his dream. With the end of the school year and coming of spring they both quit their jobs and made plans to join the show for the 1962 season.

Dale's sister, Margret, flew to California to make the trip east with them, which went via Seattle to visit the worlds fair. That fair had a unique wheel story as well. Although the Space Needle was and is, probably, the defining structure of that fair, the Giant Seattle wheel was certainly the defining midway attraction. Dale missed seeing the Seattle wheel, however, because, like Ferris's wheel in Chicago, the Seattle wheel was about a month late. When it did arrive the Velare brothers wheel ushered in a new era of the carnival business – the portable spectacular ride.

Curtis and Elmer Velare were true pioneers in outdoor show business. They were there and helped Buffalo Bill Cody organize the Showmen's League of America in 1913. They ran their own show for a while, and in 1925 partnered with Carl J. Sedlmayr in the new Royal American Shows. McKennon rates this partnering as, "one of the ten most important events in the history of collective amusement business". In its glory, the Royal American Shows was the greatest travelling midway ever produced and has never been equaled. Midways have had more rides, grossed more money, had more games, but in terms of raw glamour and having the "stuff" legends are made of they were and remain the gold standard. In 1935 the

Velare brothers left the road, and begin to operate in parks in California. It was there (in Long Beach) that they developed the double Ferris wheel or the "Space Wheel". This introduced a portable spectacular ride to the carnival business and changed everything. It wasn't long before carnival owners had to compete with each other not with just more rides, but kinds of rides, namely spectacular rides.

It was at the Seattle Worlds Fair that 77 year-old Elmer and 81 year-old Curtis introduced their Giant Seattle Wheel. They both personally supervised the setting up of the ride. Curtis ran the ride himself many hours during the fair. While the fair waited for its wheel, Wayne Kunz brought in a double skywheel from his father's (Al Kunz) Century 21 Shows for the first few weeks of the fair. Like Ferris' wheel, once it got open the Velare wheel was a huge success, carrying 662,000 riders before the end of the fair.

Dale, Alicia and Margret continued eastward on US 12 across Washington, Idaho, Montana and South Dakota to join the show in Hutchinson, Minnesota at the Hutchinson Water Carnival.

With some help from Dale's dad, they purchased a new travel trailer and had it waiting for them in Ogden when they arrived. Little did Alicia realize that her job (part of her job, at least) would be to drive the car and pull the trailer from spot to spot. It never occurred to Dale to ask if she had ever thought she could pull a trailer. That is just what the women on the show did. Some were better drivers than others. Some drove big trailers while some drover smaller ones. Some could park and back up and some couldn't. It didn't matter. The women drove the house and followed their husband's truck. With a new trailer hitch on the 1962 Chevy Alicia and Dale went to Ogden to pick up their new trailer. It was a 24 foot, rear bedroom, not self-contained Peerless. It did have a bathroom with a shower and an electric refrigerator in the kitchen. The young couple had a new home, and they were in show business. With a couple of practice laps around the block, and a couple of nervous tears down her cheeks Alicia was an official carny wife. Over the next thirty-five years she went on to drive a motorhome and several trailers – including a forty foot London Aire pulled by a 300 hp International 4700 diesel with 100 gallon fuel tanks – gross weight 32,000 pounds. Nothing, however, was quite as scary as pulling that first house trailer.

The remainder of the 1962 season went fairly smoothly. Dale set up, tore down and operated the Loop-O-Plane and Alicia sold tickets. Each night, after closing, Alicia completed the report sheet for the day's business and paid the office the percentage and sales tax due. Dale also worked on the show owned rides (mainly the wheels) for which he was paid a salary of $100 per week. On August 21, 1962 – the second day of Hobo Days in Britt, Iowa - Dale rode 854 riders on the Loop, and had the biggest day of the season. Single tickets were 35 cents.

The Platte County Fair at Columbus, Nebraska was always a favorite each year. In 1962 the dates were August 28 – 31 – Tuesday through Friday. That year Bud Butler booked his flashy, new B & H Umbrella kiddie ride into Columbus to add to the ride list. He had also played Britt, but otherwise had the ride booked with the Art B. Thomas Shows. Al Merriam was jealous of his ride gross and rarely booked independent rides. On the third day of the fair, just about sundown, storm clouds developed and were pushed in from the northwest by a straight, hard wind. Some warnings were evident and precautions were taken. Game concessions were closed and tents staked down. The midway closed and the ticket sellers brought the tickets and change bags to the office. The side wall on the merry-go-round was probably left rolled up so any wind could blow through the ride with less chance of causing damage. Standard procedure for the wheels was to remove five seats (out of the twelve total on each wheel) from the top of the ride thus lowering the center of gravity and wind resistance.

With all the usual precautions having been taken there was nothing to do now except wait out the storm. If it blows over the show will re-open and some of the night's business can be salvaged. The Merriam family – Al, Edna, Margret, Dale and Alicia – all huddled in the show's 18 foot office trailer, more for companionship than safety. This was going to be a bad one all right, but wind storms had been survived in the past and survive this one they would. Just as the rain increased in intensity and the wind subsided a bit a loud excited knock rattled the whole side of the trailer.

"The wheels are down! The wind blew the wheels down" the messenger said. "Al, come quick!" First there was disbelief and silence. Then Al and Dale scrambled for rain coats in the tight quarters. They walked the 800 feet from the office to the wheel location with their eyes still looking upward. After all, those 50 foot diameter wheels were upright when Dale last saw them. It just doesn't make sense that they would be lying in a pile – one wheel on top of the other. The merry-go-round pulled through with little or no damage. Two ticket boxes had blown over" The top was off the Loop ticket box and lying about ten feet away. Then Al and Dale saw the two wheels. They had tipped over north to south with one wheel almost on top of the other. At the entrance to each wheel (at least where the entrances used to be) were five seats neatly sitting in a row in front of each wheel. Of the seven seats remaining on each wheel many were damaged. Some hanging precariously some ten feet in the air. When the south most wheel came over it just creased the back corner of the girl show man's house trailer. As best could be seen in the dark, spokes were bent – some at 90 degree angles – seats were broken, wind braces were twisted having given up the fight trying to live up to their name. Oddly enough they still resembled Ferris wheels, albeit horizontal and one on top of the other.

Bud Butler's new umbrella ride also took a bad hit. The beautiful and colorful, 30 foot diameter top was inside out and pushed straight up into the air like a cartoon umbrella in a comic strip. By this time it was dark, wet and much too much debris was on the midway to consider re-opening. There was nothing more to be done that night. No one was sure what was to be done in the morning, for that matter. This was a major hit. The show had lost its signature twin wheels at one of its biggest fairs. For his solution, Bud – forever the optimist – took his whole crew to the Nite and Day Café which was the local 24 hour truck stop on US Highway 30 in Columbus. Alicia and Dale also went to the Nite and Day and joined the Butler crew for a late night snack. Al and Edna went to their trailer and to bed. Before sleep over took Al's thoughts that night a recovery plan had started to formulate. The details of that plan would be revealed in the morning. After all, "Tomorrow is another day".

Ironically that line would not be uttered on the silver screen that night in Columbus. On that stormy night the drive-in movie screen blew down – taken by the same wind that took the wheels. The film playing was "Gone With the Wind".

Carnival transportation in the 30's. Edna Merriam
standing by open truck door.

Two merry-go-round horses carved by Web Merriam.

Eyerly loop-o-plane renamed the Atom Smasher by
Al & sign painter friend, Marlon Balcer.

Web Merriam's first Kiddie Car ride.

Some of the rideboys in front of the Smith Chair-o-plane.

Grandpa Web telling Dale, "some day son, this will all be yours".

Web's second ride. A ten-horse pony ride with jumping horses.
Dale remembers watching his Grandfather off-set the axels
in the wheels, under the horses, to make them jump.

The Merriam's first merry-go-round. Note the name on the
ticket box, the picture had to be taken 1947 or 1948.

A mechanical show circa 1950. Note, carnival worker in a
three- piece suit, and straw hat – those were the days.

Patsy! They shake it to the East, and they shake it to the West, but come and see Patsy, she shakes it the best.

Carny Kid, Eugene Henderson standing on top a wooden junction box. Coming up behind him is Web's Miniature Train which he passed onto Dale in his will. Note, absence of fence. What keeps the Children from walking in-front of the train?

Bob Robinson elaborate Corn game.

The new 1948 Allan Herschell merry-go-round, and a new 1948 Ford truck.

Cundiff's cook house. Seated at the front counter, is show owner Al Merriam. Standing behind hot dog counter is Whitey, who proclaimed the merits of his footlongs as, "a loaf of bread, a pound of meat, and all the chili you can eat". Seated at the end counter, is Dale's Grandfather, Web, second from the front. Owned by Red and Florence Cundiff, the cook house served full meals from breakfast to dinner, and then about six o clock, switched over to full grab, and Whitey sold his hot dogs.

Another picture of the new merry-go-round. Note, still no fence?

Web's newest eight horse pony cart ride. Two number Twelve, Eli Bridge Co. wheels add flash to the backend. No fence around pony cart ride?

Columbus Nebraska, 1962, a straight hard wind blew down both wheels.

Ken Davis's trailer mounted Bingo. Hammond electric organ occupies front of trailer where Ken conducted nightly concerts before each opening.

Dale and Alicia's Loop-O-Plane.

Al and Edna Merriam

Merriam Family and Crew

CHAPTER III

THE MISSING DECADE

When the Merriam family woke up to face the new day – the last day of the Platte County Fair, August 31, 1962 – they were entering a new era for the family and the show. Alicia had completed the cashier's daily report for the previous day's business. The Loop had sold 35 tickets for a gross of $12.25. The office's percentage was $2.45, and this amount was paid. On the top of the report sheet she wrote, "Wind – Rain – Columbus – The night the wind blew and the wheels came down!" What was to be done about the two wheels? First, they had to be removed from the fairgrounds – that was for sure. Second, six more weeks remained on the route, including the new fairs in Missouri and Arkansas – Dexter, Missouri and Harrisburg, Arkansas, and a good first impression was important at those dates.

When Al got up that Friday morning he had a plan. First, the problem of removing the two damaged wheels would be dealt with. Hubert Heeren (the wheel foreman), the two men under Hubert, Dale, of course, and a young man who was visiting Dale's sister, Margret, were given the task of tearing down the two wheels and loading them in their respective trailers.

Actually, at this point, the term "tearing down" didn't quite apply. They were "down"! One wheel almost directly on top of the other. But, to the trained eye they still resembled Ferris wheels, and Hubert, Dale and their crew set to their task. The same pins and fasteners had to be removed. The same parts had to be taken off and loaded in their respective trailers. It should be noted that neither special tools nor equipment was required other than that required for normal tear down. No steel was cut nor heated with a torch to be removed. No saws of any kind were required. No fork lifts, cranes nor power equipment of any kind was required. The work went on in a quiet, almost respectful manner. As small groups of by-standers would gather to watch and comment about the damage.

Under Al's ever watchful eyes a cursory inventory was being taken of what parts were damaged, repairable, would likely need to be replaced, etc. Of the twenty-four wooden seats about half of them received some, if not considerable damage. Five seats from each wheel had been removed before the storm, as was customary. This precaution was taken every night regardless of the weather. Those seats received very little or no damage. Each part had to be taken off one at a time. Some of the spokes and other longer pieces were bent at right angles. These pieces had to be "cold" straightened by wedging one end in the truck frame and several men pushing on the other end until they could be loaded in the semi-trailer. By mid-afternoon, Dale and Hubert had the two wheels loaded in their respective trailers, parked behind the midway, pointed east and ready for the next step in the recovery plan.

Of course the show opened, as scheduled, at 1:00 PM for the last day of the fair - if a bit ragged looking. No one ever thought about nor considered not opening on time as advertised. This is show business, after all, and the fact that half of it blew away in a wind storm had little or nothing to do with opening or not. The merry-go-round music, which signaled that the show was open, during those years, was played from 45 RPM records. The merry-go-round foreman was Robert Romaine (Bobby) Arbuckle – he acquired the nickname, Rodeo Bob in later years –, and it was Bobby who had started the tradition of playing the first few bars of Gene Autry's, "Back in the Saddle Again" as the signal that the show was open. Those first few opening chords strummed on Gene's guitar had an effect no military bugle could match. Bobby was not one to spare the volume, and he was precise. When that familiar music started grown men have been seen running to their ride wiping unshaved lather from their face with their shirt sleeve and re-setting their watch at the same time. The girl show didn't open because of damaged canvas, some of the games didn't open and, of course, there was that huge gaping hole in the back end where the two wheels once stood. The cashier's report from the Loop-O-Plane that last day records that it was windy, cloudy and rained at 10:30 PM. The Loop sold 340 tickets at 35 cents and grossed $119.00. The office was paid $23.80.

By the time Hubert and Dale had the two damaged wheels loaded and parked awaiting the next step in the recovery plan, that step was revealed. Al had called the Eli Bridge Company and ordered a new #5 wheel. In 1962 it wasn't uncommon for a ride manufacturer – especially Eli Bridge – to have a ride or two in inventory, completed, or at least nearly so, and ready to ship. The decision to purchase a slightly smaller No. 5 wheel (by 5 feet) is somewhat of a curious one. Edna questioned the wisdom of that choice knowing how proud Al was when he could boast that his two wheels were bigger than any show's in his area. After all, this is show business and a little boasting is not only acceptable it's almost expected. Anyway, the decision was made and a new No. 5 it would be. It would be easier to move, easier to find a used one to pair with it next year, the fair going public probably could not tell the difference, and there was one on the factory floor in Jacksonville ready to go to work.

The next step in the plan would involve Dale, Alicia, Hubert and (again) Loren Roe – rural mail carrier, Shriner, and Al's good friend in Ogden. First the show had to be moved from Columbus to Schuyler, Nebraska for the Labor Day spot – a short 18 miles east on US 30. Schuyler (pronounced "sky – ler" even though Dale's grandfather, Wilbur, pronounced it "shoe – ler") filled the Labor Day slot on Merriam's route for many years. Located in the flat and fertile Platte River valley and on the route of the Union Pacific - as part of the first transcontinental railroad – Schuyler is in Colfax County, and named after Schuyler Colfax. Colfax was Grant's vice-president for his first term, and an active politician during the planning and building of the trans-continental railroad. Columbus ended on Friday, August 31 and Schuyler began the next day on Saturday, September 1. This required an 'overnight jump', but with only 18 miles to travel it was a very 'make-able' jump. The fact that the two wheels were already in the trucks now became an advantage. The show opened with a kiddie matinee, and the Loop sold 96 tickets at a quarter. The matinee gross was $24 and the office was paid $6.

Interestingly, it was Hubert who showed the most outward effect of the downed wheels. Maybe it was the disruption of his routine, or maybe genuine empathy for the show's loss. Whatever the reason, Hubert used set up day in Schuyler to get slightly drunk in the Tiny Bubbles bar in downtown Schuyler. He was not "roaring drunk", just slurring his words, acting belligerent, not at all effective during set up. The Tiny Bubbles bar was also partly to blame just for being there. Every town on the route has some unique landmark or characteristic that makes it identifiable and special. It might be a certain truck-stop, a certain restaurant, a lake, etc. In Schuyler, aside from the fun factoid about its name, the Tiny Bubbles was a Schuyler landmark.

The Tiny Bubbles was an interesting little saloon, and occupied a warm spot in the hearts of many on the Merriam's crew during those middle decades – the sixties and seventies. It sat on a downtown street adjacent to the midway area, and within easy walking distance of the midway and the carnival camping area. Each year the bar owner would complain bitterly to the city officials, the Labor Day celebration committee, and to Al about how the carnival took up his parking, reduced the traffic driving past his establishment, and generally hurt his business. And, every year he would come to the carnival office throughout the weekend to buy coins and one dollar bills and announce he was having such a busy day he could not keep up. Edna, or whoever was in the show office at the moment, would cheerfully give him change, listen to his complaint, and wish him well as he went back to his busy bar. Apparently, he saw no connection between the carnival midway and the festival bringing crowds of people to town and his bar having a really busy weekend.

As a result of Hubert's drinking, Al was pretty mad – probably rightly so -, and almost ready to fire him and send him home. It was Edna who prevailed, as she often did when common sense was needed to overcome "knee jerk" bad judgment calls. Al "sucked it up", Hubert sobered up, life went on, and the plan continued to unfold.

The next day, Sunday, with Al and Hubert back on speaking terms, Alicia took Dale and Hubert back to Columbus to get the two trucks and drive them to Ogden, Iowa. She would follow the trucks in Dale's and her 1962 Chevrolet Impala and bring the drivers back to Schuyler. Ogden is also on US 30 a short 200 miles east of Columbus. After the obligatory stop at the Missouri Valley, Iowa truck stop on US 30 going down the hill on the east side of town –one of Dale's favorite truck stops, and one he would never pass up – the two loads arrived in Ogden. The two men plus Loren unloaded one wheel in the winter quarters building in Ogden and made the truck ready for the trip to Jacksonville. After bidding Loran good luck and a safe trip, Alicia, Dale and Hubert returned to Schuyler. Whoever ran the Loop on Sunday in Schuyler isn't recorded, but Alicia completed the sheet for the day. One hundred-ninety-three tickets were sold for a gross of $67.80 and the office was paid $16.89. Now it was off to Slater, Missouri and the six spots that were to make up the southern route in Missouri and Arkansas.

The remaining route that year (1962) was Slater, MO Sept. 6 - 8, Piggot, AR Sept. 13 – 15, Dexter, MO Sept. 18 – 22, Harrisburg, AR Sept. 25 – 29, Hoxie, AR Oct. 1 – 6, New Madrid, MO Oct. 8 – 13. Three of these dates Dale played the year before with the now defunct Sunset Amusement Company. The other three - Piggot, Hoxie and New Madrid – Al booked to fill in the route. Al was never one to leave a date unfilled. His logic was, "The stuff won't make any money on the truck", and with that philosophy went on to find some really good two and three day, first of the week spots. He saw no reason not to apply that philosophy just because the show was a few hundred miles south of its comfort zone.

Loren Roe and the new wheel arrived in Slater from Jacksonville, Illinois about mid-morning of set up day. The timing could not have been more perfect. The excitement of seeing the shiny new ride set up for the first time spread though out the show, so when Hubert and Dale began to set up the new wheel - which they did almost immediately - most other work stopped, and a small crowd gathered around the new wheel. When it was time to install the spokes, Dale "worked the top" and Hubert "pulled ropes" just as it should have been.

This was still a ground model wheel to be trailer mounted by Al 10 years later in his winter quarters.

Paste the pic here with a caption underneath of it.

What the crew wasn't prepared for was how precise and tight all the parts fit together on the newly manufactured wheel. When pinning the spokes to the hubs, Dale was accustomed to crying out, "shake it" to the spoke tailers, and driving the hub pin in place with a sharp slap with the heel of his leather gloved right hand. With the new pins, a few healthy blows with a ball peen hammer was required. About this time, Al walked by, and was not at all pleased with Dale beating on his new wheel with a hammer. His instructions were hollered up to Dale with words to the effect, "Put some oil on those pins. They have to come out Saturday night, you know". Dale realized his error and took the oil can up with him for the next set of spokes – the top man went up and down the tower for each set – and left the hammer behind.

The remainder of the 1962 season was without major mishap. Hoxie, Arkansas was the last week in September with one more week to go in New Madrid, Missouri. It looked like a long ways back to Ogden and winter quarters, so Al decided to send the Tilt-A-Whirl and the ground model Miler coaster home from Hoxie. That would eliminate three trucks and drivers from the final jump home. Dale went north with the trucks leaving Alicia in Hoxie to sell tickets on the Loop and help with the office work. The trip went well, but Dale missed the gypsy cabbage roll dinner that Alicia remembered and talked about for years after.

By now it was the last of September, school had started, and there was no reason to open the show before about 6:00 o'clock in the evening. With this free time available, the gypsy family, Sam and Molly Evans, invited the whole show to an afternoon, cabbage roll, dinner and party. As far as their official capacity on the show, it was enough to say they were the gypsies. That meant the women (in this case, Molly) read palms and told fortunes in the Mitt Camp, Sam did odd jobs for Al. Sam never did any real work, of course, but he would run errands to town, pay the extra help on set-up and tear-down, "patch" minor complaints, etc. They also had a teenage son, Johnny and daughter that looked entirely too white. Alicia suspected she had been stolen as a baby, but who knows. The Mitt Camp, of course, was the tent or booth where Molly would tell your fortune by reading the lines on the palms of your hands – palm, hand, mitt – hence, Mitt Camp. Chapter IX will have more to say about some of these terms – like Mug Joint, Jingle Board, etc.

The weather was hot in northeast Arkansas, but Molly's cabbage rolls were hotter. She worked all morning cooking and preparing the meal. By custom, the hosts did not eat with the guests but rather, did the serving and watched with delight as the meal was enjoyed. Water, big platters of cabbage rolls and a whole loaf of sliced white bread still in the wrapper were on each table. One bite of the cabbage roll and the diner couldn't wait to grab a slice of bread from the center of the table followed by a water chaser. Bread, water, anything to extinguish the fire that burned all the way from mouth to stomach. After the initial shock and the fire subsided, the guests realized how good these delicacies were, and wiping the sweat from their brows dug in for the next bite always keeping that cooling bread within easy reach.

Margie Spurgeon, a former professional lady wrestler but now married to the show electrician, Kenny Spurgeon, asked Molly if she had and would share her recipe. Now it was unlikely that a written recipe existed, and maybe unlikely that Molly could read or write. She was, however, willing to share culinary secrets with Margie. She began to rattle off a list of ingredients like, "a few heads of cabbage, a 'leetle' hot pepper, a 'leetle' salt, rice, meat, etc. And then the final ingredient, Molly said, with a slight twinkle in her eye and an exaggerated Eastern European accent, "A quart of 'geen' (gin)". Waiting just moments for these last words to be heard and looks of disbelief, she quickly explained, "the 'geen' is for the 'kook'". Alicia has made cabbage rolls of her own since then, but she says never the equal of Molly's in Hoxie, Arkansas. Maybe she didn't use enough 'geen'.

For the five days in Hoxie, Arkansas the Loop grossed $126.35 for which the office was paid $31.58. The 1962 season ended the following week in New Madrid, Missouri. Upon arrival in the Ogden, Iowa winter quarters Dale and Alicia parked their trailer in Al and Edna's backyard and set up housekeeping with no particular long range plan in mind. After the trucks and rides were stored for the winter – some in the show owned Ogden buildings and some in the eight miles away, show owned Pilot Mound buildings – Hubert and Dale remained on the payroll to help rebuild the two downed wheels. A set of wooden wheel seats was found for sale in Illinois. These added to what could be recovered from the wreck provided two complete sets. Pieces were carefully examined, straightened, welded, painted and repaired. Some parts had to ordered from Eli Bridge, such as a set of bearing blocks (part no. Eli No.10) for two of the top towers. In a couple of weeks time, largely because of Al's skill and hard work and the expertise of Uncle Snort's machine shop, both wheels were repaired and made operational. They were subsequently sold to small amusement parks, but as far as is known never went on the road again.

With that task completed Dale and Alicia were faced with somewhat of a reality check. Though he grew up in the business, Dale was unfamiliar with an age old carnival adage known as the "three no's". They are <u>No</u> Spots, <u>No</u> Money and <u>No</u> vember.

It wasn't long before the young married couple began to have second thoughts about the occupation and the life style they had chosen. The prospect of a long, cold Iowa winter spent in the cramped confines of a twenty-six foot travel trailer was not appealing. The rental property available in Ogden (population 1500) was, also, unappealing as were the employment opportunities. Once reality hit, the couples plans fell into place fairly quickly. This was 1962, and the country had recently elected a young, enthusiastic president. The space race was in full gallop, and a big demand existed for both teachers and engineers. Alicia and Dale decided to break the bonds of the three no's and explore possibilities in "real world". In order to take advantage of the recruiting and interviewing facility at Iowa State University they moved their trailer to a trailer park in Ames.

As the fall season became winter another interesting thing happened. It got cold. Cold enough to freeze water. Cold enough to freeze water coming into the trailer and, even more troublesome. water going out. Most mornings it was just a manner of waiting until the combination of sunshine and the electrical warming tape wrapped around the water pipes melted the ice. The outgoing waster was a bit more of a problem. If one forgot and flushed too soon it was over the top and under the bed where Alicia stored her hats. If there was ever a reason against the fashion of women wearing hats, this was it. it was yell, scramble, mop and get all the hat boxes from the under bed storage to some place high and dry. Necessity has a way of realigning priorities in life, and for Alicia and Dale the priorities became staying warm, keeping the hats dry and visiting the recruiting bulletin boards at Iowa State.

It wasn't long – sometime the first part of January 1963 – Dale was interviewed by a recruiter from McDonnell Aircraft in St. Louis, Missouri. The young couple knew nothing about St. Louis, but it looked okay on the map, and with any luck, they might find somewhere to live where they could flush in the morning without checking the outside temperature first. A brief interview trip cinched the deal, and Dale accepted an industrial engineering job manufacturing Phantom F-4 fighter airplanes. A flurry of activity took place the remainder of January, including Al and Dale driving to Pine Island to get some more of Alicia's "stuff". Among that "stuff" was Alicia's piano, which Al and Dale hauled in the back of an open pick-up from Pine Island to the Merriams' house in Ogden. Dale remembers that it was a beautiful, clear and crisp day, but bitter cold. When they left for Pine Island on the 450 mile round trip journey, it was about fifteen below zero cold. It didn't really warm up all day. When it is that cold there is no sag at all in the telephone wires as they stretch from pole to pole along the two lane Iowa roads of the time. Dale imagined that when they arrived back in Ogden the cold must have tuned Alicia's piano about three octaves higher than normal. In Pine Island the instrument had to be moved down a narrow stairway from Ahneman's second floor apartment to the street. Once again the face of a small, mid-western town showed its neighborly disposition. Arnie (Alicia's father) simply walked a couple of doors down the street to the Rainbow Café, saw two men having their late morning coffee and asked if they would help move a piano. With that the piano was moved, and the Rainbow Café played another role in Dale and Alicia's lives. The piano, by the way, survived that move, the one to St. Louis, the one to Tempe, Arizona and four moves within that city to its present home at Trissa's (Dale and Alicia's daughter) home in Chandler, Arizona.

With Al's influence and help their house trailer was returned to the dealer. It was January 1963, and Dale and Alicia were officially "off the road". It was now a matter waiting for the moving van to get their "stuff" before beginning a new phase of their lives. It did not seem to be much of a concern, at the time, that their "stuff" included no furniture at all – not a bed, not a table, not even a folding chair. What they did possess, however, was that treasure that most young couples starting new lives possess, namely, energy and enthusiasm. I wasn't long before they had rented a two-bedroom, unfurnished, ground floor apartment in Bridgeton, Missouri – a short commute for Dale. The "no furniture" problem was soon solved, thanks to generous monetary gift from Alicia's folks. The first item purchased was a king-sized mattress. By putting the mattress on the floor, and rolling up the mattress carton for a sofa, the first night in their new home was – well – homey.

The St. Louis – McDonnell experience lasted from February 1963 until June 1965. It was a busy time for the aircraft industry, and for much of it Dale worked a fifty-four hour week. Alicia got a teaching job the next fall and taught kindergarten two years in nearby St. Ann, Missouri. During this time, the single most important thing that happened was meeting and becoming good friends with Brad and Rosie Bowker. That friendship has lasted over fifty years and continues today. The first meeting took place one cold, snowy February morning as Dale was going to his car parked in back of their apartment building. It might have been Dale's first official day on the job. It was certainly one of the first. Another man, obviously also, going to work was attempting to start his car without result. A conversation was struck and discoveries made that they were both industrial engineers, in the same department and new on the job. Brad was from North Dakota State in Fargo, and had been on the job a couple of weeks. Dale gave Brad a ride to work that morning while Brad shared his veteran – of two weeks – knowledge of working for McDonnell. The Bowkers' apartment was in the same four-plex – second floor, opposite corner. The first visit Brad and Rosie made to the Merriam residence probably involved sitting on the rolled up mattress carton, makeshift sofa.

Dale stayed abreast of the carnival business with letters, phone calls and two or three visits to Ogden that spring during which time he studied and became a Third Degree Mason. Winter quarters work began in Ogden about the last week in March as the first, brave robins pecked at the frost covered grass each morning bringing promising signs or spring yet to come. Rides were painted, trucks were started, wiring repaired and a used No. 5 wheel was purchased to stand beside the one that had been delivered to Slater, Missouri the previous fall. One wheel just wasn't enough. Besides Dale, one person missing that spring of 1963 was Hubert. It seems that over the winter he shot his wife, Wanda. The altercation was not fatal, but in Iowa, at least, it was illegal. Hubert missed the 1963 and most of the 1964 seasons. He returned in either the 1965 or 1966 seasons more mature and with a new wife, Lois. Lois sold tickets for a while, but quickly advanced to working in the show office giving Edna some much needed help. It might be pointed out that Lois was some skinnier than Wanda, and thus, a smaller target.

Also, during this time Dale and Alicia still owned the Loop-O-Plane ride. Al agreed to take the Loop on the road at the usual rate plus operating and moving expenses plus wages for one man and one ticket seller. This worked to both parties good giving some income to Dale and Alicia and the additional ride for the show. Financing had been arranged to pay for the ride over three seasons – 1961, 1962 and the current season, 1963.

The spring and summer of 1963 passed quickly as Dale and Alicia settled into their new routine. A routine that found Dale working a 54 hour week – 7:00 A M to 4:30 P M Monday through Saturday. His engineering skills learned at Iowa State were honed and refined on the assembly line t McDonnell Aircraft. He also developed a great respect and appreciation for the precise and skilled workmanship of the men and women who actually drilled the holes, drove the rivets and shaped the metal building F-4 Phantom fighter airplanes. Years later he would meet retired Air Force pilots (pardon, he would be corrected, that's fighter pilots) who would thank him for his part in building such a fine airplane. By the time fall came around Alicia had a job teaching kindergarten in nearby St. Ann, Missouri. She kept that job the next year as well, and faithfully banked every pay check in a savings account at First Federal Savings in Des Moines, Iowa.

The St. Louis years were good ones for Dale and Alicia, but they both knew this was not to be their permanent life style. Dale was interested in graduate school as a way of advancing in his profession, and they both had a desire to travel before "settling down" – whatever that meant. Lyndon Baines Johnson was sworn in as the 36th President having won a landslide victory over his conservative opponent, Barry Goldwater. Far reaching social changes took place in the country as he declared "war on poverty" and ushered in "the great society". Dale applied and was accepted by the graduate school programs at both Arizona State University and the University of Oklahoma while, at the same time, the young couple made plans to take a month off for a thirty day trip to Europe – Alicia had that two years of teaching salary -"banked" for the occasion. When the head of the industrial engineering department at Arizona State called and offered Dale a $1,200 research assistantship decisions were made and the plan quickly fell into place. They would both quit their jobs, go to Europe for a month, come back to Missouri to get their "stuff" and simply move to Arizona. The obvious gaps and details of the plan would be filled in later as could only be done with the energy and enthusiasm of a couple in love and in their twenties.

Meanwhile, the show was getting ready for its seventeenth season. The

1965 route card listed 33 spots beginning with Perry, Iowa May 6-7-8 and ending with Wardell, Missouri October 11 – 16. The ride list was:

Two No. 5 Eli Wheels
Merry-go-round
Oct-o-pus
Tilt-a-whirl
King car ride
King pony carts (with Wilbur's ponies and carts)
Loop-o-plane
Scrambler
Kiddie coaster

It was during this time that the show was probably the most far away from Dale's mind it ever was or would be. Far from his mind, maybe, but his heart was another matter. That feeling became evident once during the summer of 1964 when Alicia was experiencing impacted wisdom teeth problems. When her dental problems became complicated by lung problems it was decided that she should go back to Pine Island and the familiar ground of the Mayo clinic – just eighteen miles away. Alicia flew to Minnesota to begin the process of having her lung examination, and Dale was to follow in a few days. The lung diagnosis histoplasmosis commonly contacted by people living near the central and lower Mississippi River. There is no real cure. It's something one just gets over. The scary part is that the symptoms, at least on the x-ray film, resemble tuberculosis. The plan was for Dale to fly to Rochester and be with Alicia in the hospital when she had her wisdom teeth extracted. The day before he was to leave, Dale was startled when his desk phone rang and it was his mother. The show was in Missouri Valley, Iowa at the Harrison County Fair and moving to Columbus, Nebraska next. She knew he was planning to take a few days off work and go to Minnesota, but could he make a little side trip on the way? Both wheels were up in Missouri Valley, they had no wheel man, and they were one driver short to make the jump. Hubert was in Iowa and could tear them down, but he couldn't leave the state. The Iowa Department of Corrections still had him on a short leash for shooting Wanda. The sense of adventure and the recollection of the feel of 7/8's rope in his hands as the towers were raised into place were just too much for him to think straight. After all, Alicia was in the able care of her mother and the Mayo Clinic. He changed his airline tickets, flew to Omaha, got picked up, drove a semi to Columbus and the next day set up two wheels in the exact location where the two No. 12 s blew over two years before. The next day he flew on to Rochester to be with Alicia (minus 4 wisdom teeth). Alicia and her mother – as one would expect – were a bit angry at Dale's lack of good judgment.

With the end of the school year 1965, things started to happen pretty much as planned. First, 31 days in Europe on a tour bus for a trip Dale and Alicia would remember the rest of their lives After returning to New York they visited the World's Fair in that city - their second world's fair in three years. Next would be a stop in Minnesota to visit Alicia's folks in Pine Island, and then to Detroit Lakes, Minnesota to visit the show there and make the jump to Cambridge before returning to St. Louis to get their "stuff". Getting the "stuff" was more of a challenge now, largely because there was simply more "stuff". But somehow they rented a U-Haul truck and Dale got it all snuggly packed inside – piano and all. With more dreams than plans and a quick backward glance they were off to Arizona. Dale drove the truck and Alicia followed in their '65 Buick Wildcat. In their rearview mirrors they could see the famous St. Louis arch not quite completed. The two sides were almost at full height awaiting the placement of the connecting topmost piece of the arch. There it would stand to honor explorers Meriwether Lewis and William Clark just as Ferris's wheel did after being moved from Chicago to the 1903 world's fair held in St. Louis.

Three days later they were in Tempe, Arizona, and it was HOT! They knew it might be a little warm. It was summer, after all, and this was the Arizona desert. But, it was HOT. They were fifteen-hundred miles from the nearest family or friends. Dale had a $1,200 assistantship and no other source of income; they had no place to live; they were paying daily rent on the truck that contained their "stuff" and it was HOT! Suddenly the three-no's became <u>no money</u>, <u>no house</u> and <u>no escaping the heat.</u> But, Dale had two valuable assets which would save the day. The first was no more tangible than that he was lucky at just the right time. The second (and perhaps the more important) was that he was married to Alicia who had taken the precaution of having her teaching credentials transferred to Arizona. It wasn't long before these two assets began to pay off.

The first month was awful, but there was so much to do, so many things to become accustomed to (like the 100-plus degree weather), and new people to meet that it passed fairly quickly. They moved twice the first month from one unbearable hovel of an apartment to another before they found a nice two-bedroom house within a bicycle ride from the ASU campus. Dale got registered in the Industrial Engineering Master's program, and immediately developed a friendship with Lee Searcy, the Assistant to the Dean of Engineering. Alicia interviewed for and got a job offer to teach kindergarten in the nearby Guadalupe School District. Her interviewer, realizing Alicia was new to Arizona, casually mentioned the children were largely bilingual. Alicia, having taught in California, expected that, and was comfortable with it. Comfortable, that is, until the interviewer further explained that the two languages were Spanish and Yaqui Indian. The challenge never came to be, however, because another teaching offer came from the Scottsdale District, and it was quickly accepted. They were set. With a house, Dale registered in graduate school and a newly purchased bicycle for transportation, Alicia with a new teaching job and a 1965 Buick Wildcat for transportation, they were ready to settle down to their "work-day, study-day" new life. With a few days before the beginning of the school year they took a short trip back to Southern California to see their old haunts and visit Alicia's Aunt Ruth and Uncle Bill. Then it was back to school - teach, study, learn, and meet wonderful new lifetime friends. Each day Dale would ride his bicycle north on College Avenue to ASU and watch the activity of the new post office being built at College and Southern. The building activity on campus was a new library. Dale completed his Master's program in one academic year, and was accepted into the PhD program. Alicia's parents, Arnie and Hilda, closed their beauty shop in Pine Island for a couple of months and rented an apartment in Tempe with an eye toward retiring. More new friends were met, and Dale and Alicia were feeling they had found their home. The population of Tempe was about 30,000.

It really seemed as if Dale had found his niche. He liked his professors, he liked sharing office space with fellow graduate students and while doing research for his master's degree, he couldn't wait for the new library to be completed. Dale and Alicia's plans were directed toward the University and Arizona lifestyle. From all appearances, owning the carnival was the furthest thing from Dale's mind. However, he still owned the loop-o-plane, which was on the show at that time and he always looked forward to his father's phone calls giving him carnival operation and new booking reports. Dale's missing decade had begun.

Back in Tempe Arizona, new opportunities seemed to present themselves just when Dale and Alicia needed them the most. Others have told Dale, that he is just "plain lucky". With the addition of baby Todd to their family, Alicia had to quit her teaching job. Just about the time Dale cashed his last paycheck from his assistantship at ASU, he was offered a full-time research job with the Center for the Study of Urban systems at ASU. This job allowed him the freedom to complete his master's degree and begin classwork for his PhD. Two years later, when the funding dried up on that research center, the college of Engineering had an opening for an operations manager at the Computer Center which again gave him academic freedom, flexible hours and close relationships with Engineering faculty.

An important factor at this same time was that Dale would get 4 weeks' vacation every year. Dale and Alicia would take these four weeks to escape the Arizona heat and spend time visiting the carnival in Iowa and Minnesota. This allowed Dale to keep abreast of the continuing changes in the carnival industry as well keeping him connected to the current state of affairs concerning his Dad's plans for retirement.

Near the end of the 1973 season, right after Dale and Alicia came back to Arizona to settle in for the fall, Al Merriam made a fateful phone call to Dale. He called Dale to tell him that he was going to sell the show. As fate would have it and as surprising as that announcement was, it happened to occur at just the right time in Dale's life. The University was planning to combine the computer center with the data processing operation and Dale wasn't sure what his job was going to be, or if he was even going to have a job. Dale was comfortable with the Department of Engineering having control over the computer center. The computer center organized under the college of Engineering was focused towards education and research. It was almost an unwritten rule that if the computer center got a program to work properly, there was almost no interest in running that program a second time. At that point, it was always about building bigger and better things.

If Dale was ever going to chart a different course in his life, perhaps now was the time. Coupled with the sense of uncertainty in Dale's career path, was some additional uncertainty in Al and Edna's life. Obviously they were not getting any younger. They had some health issues, with Al's beginning Parkinson's disease and high blood pressure. Al had a tentative buyer for the show, but new and much more exciting possibilities presented themselves. Suddenly all the pieces were starting to fit together in order for Dale and Alicia to buy the show.

That September Dale flew to Mitchell South Dakota, during the Corn Palace Festival, where, at the time, Bob Hope was playing the Corn Palace. This classic American icon played two shows a day and three on Saturday, for a total of 18 shows that week. Remarkable for an entertainer of his fame and his age. During the last week in September of 1973, Dale signed the sales agreement and the torch officially passed. The new era of Merriam's Midway Shows was about to begin.

CHAPTER IV

THE TORCH PASSES –
A CHANGING INDUSTRY

Dale and Alicia's decision to buy the show was huge and life changing with little threat of over statement. A few subtle, political things were going on at the University that caused Dale to be concerned about his career. First among these were the Universities' decision to purchase a new computer and combine the functions of education and research with those of administration. Dale had a fresh PhD in his pocket and good friends in the College of Engineering suggesting that he look for other opportunities. A wife and three children to care for would tend to tip the decision toward the good, stable university job complete with benefits. It was pretty certain the show was going to be sold. If it was now or never, maybe this is the now. Any way we all know the decision. A new office trailer was purchased. A used Hampton Space Age ride was purchased. Likewise, a bumper car ride was added to the lineup. And it was agreed that winter quarters would remain in Ogden Iowa where seasonal repairs and refurbishing would be done for the upcoming 1974 season. The bumper car ride and new office trailer were probably the most significant changes to the show. The addition of this equipment for the 1974 season quickly demonstrated that Dale was ready to take the show to the next level. The bumper cars, or "scooters", were an especially popular ride asked for by both the costumers and sponsors. One of the drawbacks was that the scooters were very labor intensive to move - a factor which kept some shows from featuring them. The office trailer and Space Age ride were purchased in Arizona. Bruce Carlson, of Ogden IA, and Paul Haugland of Belmond IA, drove Al Merriam's pick up to Arizona, along with Dale, and took this new equipment back to Ogden and the 1974 winter quarters were officially opened.

Dale couldn't have had a better teacher in his father Al when it came to winter quarters type work. Every piece of equipment that was painted aluminum was repainted for the coming season using spray guns, brushes and "paint rags". Besides painting, light fixtures were re-wired, broken welds were detected and repaired and worn parts were replaced. About a half a dozen of the experienced rideboys would report to winter quarters about the 1st of April and "winter quarters" work would be completed in about 5 weeks. Dale benefited from the experienced crew in winter quarters. Not all of the old crew returned. Hubert Heeron quit after about a week. He didn't think he'd be happy under the new organization with Dale in charge. Another worker who went by the name of Cherokee came back after a couple years absence and was put in charge of the bumper cars. Dale's no dog rule almost caused the Tilt foreman to leave, but a few days before opening in Perry IA, instead of leaving, he got rid of the dog. At the end of these five weeks the show was ready for its first opening date, Perry Iowa. And what an opening it was. The shop trailer had a flat tire on the 18 mile jump from Ogden calling for Al to call back to Ogden for someone to swing by Gunyon Supply for a spare. It seemed as if a little tire trouble on the jump was just part of the adventure making up the whole. To this he added a badly sung imitation of Kenny Rogers singing, "You picked a fine time to leave me loose wheel". Set up went reasonably well, largely due to the experience of the returning crew. That weekend the weather did what it often does in the Spring in Iowa – it rained. The first year Dale went to Iowa State he had a roommate also from Ogden whose name was Roger Tonsveldt. Roger was an Ag student. He told Dale, "there was never a rain we didn't need". While it may be true for an Ag student, Dale wasn't sure he needed this one.

With two seasons of current experience coupled with a lifetime of experience from childhood up until now, Dale was ready to put his own mark on the show. Some of these "marks" would be big and bold - like getting rid of gasoline engines on rides and changing all power to show generated electricity. Not all the ideas Dale had were good ones. For example, the idea to put electronic cash registers in the food concessions was a good idea that didn't wind up working out. Having cash registers allowed us to charge sales tax on each sale. On the surface that sounds like a good idea. However, we quickly found out a carnival food customer does not want to pay $1.29 for a corndog that used to be $1.25.

Pay one price ticketing was without a doubt the most important innovation in Carnival ride admissions in a long time and quite possibly ever. Pacific Ocean Park filled, it seemed, every available billboard in the city of Long Beach with pictures of their big coaster and their new pricing policy – POP - Pacific Ocean Park – POP Pay One Price. It was an immediate success. When Disney got rid of the "E" ticket system, they also got rid of disgruntled customers who were holding two or three "A" tickets which would be worthless unless you had enough of them. POP morphed into what we now know today as "Wristbands". Wristbands were accepted by carnival management with some caution and reluctance. It seems as if you sell a customer a ticket for unlimited rides, that they wouldn't buy any more tickets. One solution to the problem: Have the unlimited rides available for only a certain time. For example, some shows tried "Midnight Madness Sales". Unlimited ride wristbands might be good from 11pm until 3am. The Arizona State Fair in Phoenix tried the midnight madness idea with limited success. A meeting was held with all the ride owners to discuss the idea. Kiddie ride operators protested that all their customers would be at home in bed, so they were excused from participation. Many owners complained that they didn't have enough employees to work during the extra operating hours. Part way through the meeting, a side show operator in the back of the room, raised his hand to speak. He explained his show had the "Ugliest Man in the World", and he only had one ugliest man in the world. He had no way to expand his hours of operation. After a few chuckles, he also was excused from participation. It didn't take long for Carnival owners to figure out how to make wristbands successful on their shows. Wristbands have become a successful and regular part of midway marketing and Merriam's Midway Shows was no exception.

There were many other ideas implemented on Merriam's Midway Shows during the period when the torch was passed. Some seemed like good ideas but wound up not working out, while other ideas were positive. Below is a list of ideas that were implemented showing either their positive or negative impact.

Idea	Good, Bad or Medium	Reason
Employee ID badges, show shirts and hats	Good	Professional appearance
Fun Cards	Medium	Kept track, too high maintenance
Ride coupons in lieu of tickets	Good	Fewer ticket boxes
Wristbands	Good	Good customer response
Utilized scale to weigh tickets	Good	Improved accuracy
Posting ticket sales for each ride	Good	Healthy Competition
Reduced number of ticket boxes	Good	Cut down payroll
Driver's meetings	Good	Improved transportation
Tear down meetings	Good	Faster Tear Downs
Changed weekly pay to every two weeks	Good	Cut paperwork in half
No dog policy	Bad	Wasn't practical
No facial hair Policy	Good	Suggests cleanliness
Organized into 2 units	Good	Efficient use of equipment

In 1974, when the torch officially passed, Dale purchased 10 rides from his father. These were:

1. Eli Wheel
2. Merry-go-round (Alan Herschell)
3. Oct-o-pus
4. Tilt-a-whirl
5. Scrambler
6. Round Up
7. Trabant
8. Motorcycles
9. Boats
10. Super Slide

3 Rides were purchased from other sources. These were:

11. Space Age
12. Scooter
13. Moon Walk

Over the next 19 years, from 1974 – 2003 these rides were purchased:

F80
Spook Nook
Hurricane
Zipper
Thunderbolt
Spinning Apples (Todd's first purchase)
Hy 5 Wheel
SkyWheel
Kamikaze
SpinOut
Crazy Bus (Todd's 2nd purchase)
Train
Wacky Worm
Wacky Shack
Lolli Swing
Glass House
Monkey Mayhem
Panda Bears
Whales
Eli Kiddie Swings
4x4
Spider
Orbiter
Chance 3 abreast Merry Go Round
StarShip

Significant equipment upgrades and changes, during this time, include:

1 1976 Caterpillar Generator
Purchase of Food and Game concessions
Centralized, modernized air-conditioned Ticket Boxes w/ trailer

Upgraded Tilt to be loaded on one trailer
Designed new Boat ride truck
Trailer mounted the scrambler
Trailer mounted the Merry-Go-Round Center
New, metal junction boxes (old ones were wooden)
Converted all gas motors on rides to electricity
Implemented Tent for Office
Introduced Company branded Front Gate to the Midway
Introduced Customer hospitality benches
Implemented light towers
Implemented bunk houses for employees
Implemented identical canvas tops for all rides, games and
concessions

During the period of time when the torch officially passed, Dale's parents, Al and Edna could still be occasionally seen on the midway overseeing their son's progress with the show. Dale welcomed any and all advice from his father Al as he was experiencing many new challenges and obstacles to overcome.

CHAPTER V

THE GLORY YEARS (1980'S – THE END OF THE CENTURY)

In the late 70's Alicia's Dad, Arnold Ahneman, was taking tickets at Merriam's Moon Walk ride. He had a parent of a child ask this question, "Two Tickets!?? .. Why would it take two tickets to ride the Moon Walk?". Arnold's response, …. "It all started with Roosevelt".

Well.. likewise, for Merriam's Midway Shows, the glory years all started with the Thunderbolt.

The purchase of the Thunderbolt was the turning point for the show. It changed everything because the ride was so expensive that Dale was pressured to generate more money to make the payments. The decision to buy the Thunderbolt was made the year before at the Platte County Fair in Columbus NE. Dale realized if he was going to grow the show and be successful in the business, he had to take advantage of the grossing ability of the Thunderbolt's high capacity, super thrill ride. The size and cost of the ride caused Dale to book new spots that could pay for it.

The Thunderbolt was manufactured by chance Mfg Company Wichita KS which was the leading manufacturer of amusement rides in the U.S. at the time. As chance would have it, (pardon the pun), a salesman from Chance Mfg visited Merriam's Midway Shows, during the fair in Columbus in 1985. Dale and the salesman stood at the back of the midway during one of the big days of the fair, and saw the potential riders walking around the midway. Dale realized that Merriam's Midway Shows obviously needed more rides for that fair. The seed was planted for the future purchase.

The Thunderbolt was delivered to Anoka County Fair, Anoka MN in the summer of 1986. The size and scope of the ride was a bit overwhelming for the setup crew. Merriam's Rideboys were not yet used to a ride of this magnitude. But carry on they did and the mighty Thunderbolt, the behemoth that it was, made opening in all of its glory. The lights, the music, the speed and the DJ all added to the excitement of the 1986 midway.

With the addition of the Thunderbolt, not only did the show have to acquire new, larger spots, there was also added pressure to begin to acquire more spectacular rides. Merriam's purchased a Kamikaze, an Orbiter, a Starship and a SpinOut within the next 10 years, transforming the midway into the upper echelon of American Carnivals. Now, for the first time in Merriam's history, it was actually possible for the Carnival to play a state fair.

During the next decade, Merriam's played a number of very large County fairs along with two state fairs, those being South Dakota and New Mexico. During this time, the Glory years were in full swing as the total number of rides on the midway reached an all-time high of 30.

Below is a listing of the 30 rides during the Glory years:

MERRIAM'S MIDWAY SHOWS, INC.
OFFICE OWNED RIDE LIST

	NAME	MANUFACTURER	YEAR	SERIAL NO.
1	TILT-A-WHIRL	SELLNER MFG. CO.	1947	708
2	MERRY-GO-ROUND	ALLEN-HERSHELL	1948	H8747
3	SPIDER	EYERLY AIRCRAFT CO	1967	3506-73
4	SCOOTER(BUMPER CAR)	FLOYD & BAXTER	1966	DM1
5	BOATS	HAMPTON MFG. CO.	1966	8266
6	MOTORCYCLES	HAMPTON MFG. CO.	1967	T-9167
7	SUPER SLIDE	HRUBETZ MFG. CO.	1969	S107
8	SCRAMBLER	ELI BRIDGE CO.	1979	6-79
9	RIO GRANDE TRAIN	ZAMPERLA	1996	RG22F008US95
10	ZIPPER	CHANCE MFG. CO.	1982	82-1839R
11	KIDDIE KASTLE	PLEASURE & LEISURE	1993	93-KK
12	PANDA BEARS	VENTURE MFG. CO.	1984	14028
13	THUNDER BOLT	CHANCE MFG. CO.	1986	392-009 86
14	HY-5-II WHEEL	ELI BRIDGE CO.	1987	88-87
15	GO-GATOR	WISDOM MFG. CO.	1988	1F9DGW2T9JM063348
16	RAIDERS	WISDOM MFG. CO.	1986	1W9FRW3SOGMO81226
17	WACKY SHACK	FUNNI-FRITE	1989	OH0016389
18	STARSHIP 2000	WISDOM MFG. CO	1995	1F9GGW9T7SM063685
19	SPIN THE APPLE	SELLNER MFG. CO.	1990	SPTA-23T-90
20	SKY WHEEL	ALLEN-HERSHELL	1967	471667
21	SWING	ELI BRIDGE CO.	1984	4-84
22	CRAZY BUS	ZAMPRELA	1992	B073US92
23	KAMIKAZE	FARFABRI	1994	ZA9RAN3A146A98477
24	LOLLY SWING	ZAMPRELA	1999	LS32R076US98
25	WHALES	HAMPTON MFG. CO.	1994	RG93985
26	FOUR X FOUR	WISDOM MFG. CO.	1988	T7680R
27	CARROUSEL	CHANCE MFG. CO.	1997	404-02997
28	ORBITOR	TIVOLI (England)	1998	487230
29	KID POWER	KIDPOWER SYSTEMS	1984	KP868558
30	GLASSHOUSE	SHOW-ME MFG. CO.	1999	1H9CP3025X1280314

List of significant spots added that increased momentum for the show:

> Anoka MN
> Fergus Falls MN
> Souix City IA
> Austin MN
> Bemidji MN
> Columbus NE
> Spencer IA
> Lake City MN
> Albert Lea MN

By the time the Glory years had reached their peak, Dale was ready to sell the show to his son, Todd and Torch passed once again. Below is the ride list in 2003 when Todd Merriam became the owner of Merriam's Midway Shows:

1. High 5 Wheel
2. Merry-go-round (Alan Herschell)
3. Chance 3 abreast Merry Go Round
4. Train
5. 4x4
6. Panda Bears
7. Eli Kiddie Swings
8. Whales
9. Monkey Mayhem
10. Wacky Shack
11. Glass House
12. Crazy Bus
13. Super Slide
14. Tilt-a-whirl
15. Scooter
16. Sizzler
17. Hurricane
18. SkyWheel
19. Thunderbolt

20. Zipper
21. Kamikaze
22. Orbiter
23. SpinOut
24. StarShip

The Glory years of Merriam's Midway Shows lasted approximately 25 years, from 1980 – 2003. After Dale officially passed the torch to Todd, Dale and Alicia remained on the show for the next 13 years. Dale and Alicia's daughter, Trissa and her husband Matt, have been an integral part of the inner workings and business of the carnival. Assisting and aiding Todd in all aspects of the show. Dale continued to be a part of all operations including, teardown-setup, management, finances, driving, promotion and providing guidance where needed. Alicia worked in the office, ticket boxes, food concessions and provided catering for show parties and board committees. Dale and Alicia were on the show together from 1974 through 2016. Approximately 40 years of fun, adventure, laughs, challenges, achievements and memories. On their 50th wedding Anniversary, they took all their children and families on a Caribbean Cruise to celebrate. Dale and Alicia currently live together in Tempe Arizona and have been married for 58 years.

CHAPTER VI

THE RIDEBOYS

As the carnival industry evolved and Merriam's evolved along with it, more and more emphasis was placed on the rides and less and less on shows and exhibits. This trend would also extend to the games, later-on, as well. Carnivals were defined, as to size and importance within the industry, by the number of rides they had (carried) on their respective midways. In the fifties, perhaps, eight to twelve ride carnivals were 'medium sized', shows with twelve to twenty or more rides were 'big' shows capable of playing state fairs. By the early sixties those ride numbers had at least doubled. Fairs and the fair going public was demanding more rides to fill their midways as the number and popularity of shows declined. In the spirit of American competition carnival owners were almost eager to meet those demands. Ride manufacturers were developing and offering new and more spectacular attractions with every coming season. Joining established manufacturers like Allan-Herschell, Sellner, Eli Bridge, Eyerly and Hrubetz were new comers such as Chance Mfg in Wichita, Kansas, King Mfg. in Michigan, Hampton Mfg. in Missouri and Venture in North Carolina. Each of these contributed in their own unique way.

Chance Introduced the Trabant in 1962 and went on to produce 350 rides of that style over the next several decades. Hampton, at about the same time, produced a very popular and affordable line of super kiddie rides patterned after the B & H Umbrella ride. With their buzzers, flashing lights, and multi-colored counter rotating tops, these rides offered size and flash not seen before in "kiddie rides". King offered a wide variety of lower priced kiddie and major rides which allowed the smaller shows to "play the numbers game" and stay competitive for midway contracts.

With this increased emphasis on the number and size of rides came an increased need for a special breed of man to move them. Once again the American spirit came through, and just as the cowboy appeared on the scene at just the right time to drive herds of half wild cattle from the Rio Grande to the railroad yards of Kansas a special breed of man – the rideboy - was there to "move the iron" when the boss said, "Move it". The similarity between these occupations and the traits that made for success cannot be denied. They drank, brawled, they chased women, they were intensely loyal to their boss, and might just wander off into the sunset for no good reason at all. They could work all day and evening, tear down their ride, drive all rest of the night and morning to the next spot smelling of sweat, motor oil and coffee spilled on their already dirty shirt and still look pretty good to a starry-eyed town girl who was becoming bored with the nice farm boy who lived two miles out of town. The American cowboy has been glamorized in song and story, shown on stage and screen and became a legend and ride boy didn't because of two reasons. There were a lot more cowboys and they had better writers. Had Zane Grey traveled with a show like, perhaps, the Sunset Amusement Company John Wayne might have had another script.

In the social hierarchy of the carnival organization the ride boys didn't occupy a very high level. It's not fair to put them on the bottom because on occasion, like when a truck was stuck in the mire of a muddy fairgrounds and the dozen or so people pushing to free it included rideboys, jointees, the boss, wives, larger children and couple of barking dogs, the social strata gets a little blurred. To be accurate, however, most of the carnival occupations thought themselves a step above the rideboy. The agents in the games dressed a little nicer, got to bed (or to the local bar) earlier on teardown night, smelled better and on big spots made more money. The rideboy, on the other hand, was salaried so that in the slow spots he just might be the lender instead of the lendee. The game owners definitely thought they were better than any rideboy. Some game owners, if not most, thought of themselves as next in line to the show owner himself. They weren't, of course, but some thought it. Remember the organizations structure of the carnival – monolithic to the extreme. But the boss – who was ultimately responsible for moving the show – knew the importance of the rideboy. He was the bone, muscle, and sinew that flexed, shoved and carried to make the show move.

Within the carnival organization existed an organization of the rideboys themselves. This was a simple organization with men assigned to each ride or in some cases two or three smaller rides. Each ride had a foreman and under him a second man and then, perhaps, a third or fourth man. The hierarchy of second, third and fourth, etc. was pretty much understood as opposed to a foreman supervising a crew of equals. When, as was often the case, extra (temporary, usually local and hourly) help were hired they fell into the "crew" category. Each of the regulars had their job. For example, when the twelve spokes were pulled in place as the Eli wheel was set up the foreman *pulled ropes*, the second man *worked the top* (climbing the tower to pin the spoke in place at the hub) and a third man plus one extra help or two extra help *tailed spokes*. The foreman usually did any leveling of ride bases during set up. During teardown the second man typically *worked the truck*, that is, stayed in the truck to place or "rack" pieces of the ride as they were carried to him, leaving the foreman to direct the crew on the ground as they dismantled the ride. The foreman usually drove the truck or if it was a ride requiring two trucks he would drive the larger of the two. If he was married and had his own living quarters house trailer the wife drove the trailer and followed behind the ride truck.

It probably wasn't until about the mid-eighties that shows began furnishing show-owned living quarters for the employees. Before that the help was expected to simply make do. The organizational structure then dictated that the foreman had the first choice of living in the cab of the truck that pulled the loaded ride. If that foreman was married or had a family some creativity was required. An example of this was demonstrated on the Sunset Amusement Company (One of the few carnivals that, contrary to tradition, didn't use the word "Shows" in their company name.) They were out of Excelsior Springs, Missouri and toured from Arkansas to Minnesota. The foreman of their merry-go-round was married and had a family of three children, a dog, and enough furniture to fill a small apartment of that 1962 era.

The Sunset Amusement Company was very disciplined in the way they moved. On the last day of an event (spot), with the show closed, teardown well under way and the committee paid the owner, Ken Garman and his wife Florence, would get in Ken's Cadillac, drive to the next spot and check into a motel. Carrying no more than one night's clothes and toiletries and with lot stakes in the trunk of the Cadillac, Mr. Garman would have the lot completely laid out early the next morning so that ride trucks could go directly to their location and set up could begin at once. I didn't matter that some of these men had not been in bed at all. It didn't matter that it might be Monday morning and the show didn't open until Wednesday at 5:00 o'clock so there was no immediate rush. It didn't matter if it was raining, cold, windy, dusty or that it was a mid-August afternoon in southern Arkansas. What you did was set up. The thought of questioning the policy never occurred to anyone.

The merry-go-round foreman had a little more on his plate. The thirty-five foot van semi-trailer that carried his ride was also his house. All the previous week that trailer has been his and his families' house. The double bed complete with box springs and mattress were near the front of the van with a nightstand on one side complete with reading lamp. A wooden kitchen table with chairs would have been near the center and a sofa with matching ottoman rested on a, if not immaculately clean at least colorful, eight by twelve piece of carpeting. Somewhere in that collection must have been a couple of big wooden boxes to contain cooking utensils, toys, dog dishes, boots, shoes, etc. Water was in a bucket with a dipper hanging on the side and cooking was on a kerosene camp stove.

Now it's the last day of the spot. In fifties and sixties one thing that softened the schedule somewhat was that the day was divided into the afternoon matinee and the evening hours. The carnival midway would close for the supper hour, usually from 5 to 6 or 6:30. Aside from taking a break, resting and grabbing a bite to eat this time was used, especially on the last day, for various preparations. The second man might carry a five gallon can of gasoline and fill the ride motor for the evening's run. Electric motors eventually did away with this chore but gasoline powered rides were around well into the eighties. While his second man was carrying gas and filling the tank the foreman might be checking oil and water in the engine, greasing various bearings and moving parts on the ride, and attending to other safety and maintenance matters. House trailers were hooked up to their pulling units, tires kicked, and last- minute inventories taken of various tools and pieces of equipment needed for teardown.

It was during this time that the merry-go-round man and his family would "slough the house". Somehow the phrase, "slough the house" has a certain roughness to it as it rolls off the tongue, and that implied roughness describes the act, all the more precisely. Everything had to come out of the van; the bed, the bedding, the nightstand, the boxes full of stuff, the sofa, the kitchen table with chairs, and finally the eight by twelve carpet neatly rolled and secured with a leather strap. All placed somewhere off the midway and out of the way. Priority for the space in the van now belonged to the merry-go-round and when the last musical note floated out of the band organ in center of the ride that space was going to be claimed. About three hours after closing the merry-go-round would be neatly loaded (racked) in the semi- trailer with the families household loaded in whatever empty space was available. This was not a last minute, helter- skelter loading. Each item had its place. The table, the chairs, the roll of carpet each had its place. When the merry-go-round truck arrived at the next spot the process would be repeated in reverse. First, all the household items would be unloaded from the van. The truck would then be "put on location" and in a few hours the merry-go-round would be set up. Following this the truck would be parked where it was to stay for the duration of the spot and the families' home would be set up and made livable. On the Sunset Amusement Company's route this process would be repeated about twenty-five times during the summer.

For this the rideboy received a weekly salary plus a ten per cent bonus payable at the end of the season as long as they didn't get fired or quit somewhere along the way. In the early fifties the foreman's rate was $50 per week and $55 if they drove, second men received $40 - $45 plus $5 for driving, third men would start at $35 - $40.

The earliest rideboys I can remember (that is, remember with any vivid mental picture) are Johnny, Ronnie and Frank. Frank Chavez was the Tilt foreman and was an impeccable dresser. This was way before the time of having the ride operators uniformly dressed in show shirts. Frank would get the ride set up and always find a place to bath, shower or, otherwise, get cleaned up. Often times the right- hand mirror of one of the two Tilt trucks served as a shaving mirror. Frank liked white shoes with pastel sport shirts and slacks. His clothes always looked fairly new because it was often easier to buy new than find a cleaners or laundry facility. Ronnie Keeling was the merry-go-round man. Ronnie drove the truck, operated the ride, did the mechanical maintenance and kept the ride and himself neat and clean. Johnny Reed was the electrician and the alpha male of this three dog pack. When they were good they were really good and could move the show with apparent relative ease. The problem was that they were a "pack" and a few times they attempted to hold my father "hostage" by demanding more pay or by threatening to quit and leave the ride set up (or "in the air"). What they didn't know is that they were dealing with a man who could not be intimidated. One time I recall they asked Al what he would do if they just quit and walked off? Without blinking or hesitation my father said, "Well, I would just get on the telephone and call in my second crew." Faced with that response, they looked at one another with puzzled expressions and went back to work.

Meet some of the more storied, colorful, and memorable.

Robert Romaine (Bobby) (Rodeo Bob) Arbuckle, Jefferson Iowa

In 1953 Bobby was a skinny, nineteen year old kid with arms about the diameter of a pencil and a couple of tattoos. He must have joined in Jefferson one spring or, possibly, Perry. Perry was also often an early spring date, and he had some family connections around there. His first job was as third man on the tilt. He was never really Tilt-A-Whirl material. He was too light for the heavy lifting, and probably was intimidated by strong minded foremen like Frank Chavez and later Jerry Leeper. Leo Stuker (a big, moose of a man, if a bit slow mentally) was the resident tilt-a-whirl second man for years so the field was a bit crowded. For a few years Bob would come and go, never quite making a full season. Each time he returned, though, he was a little more seasoned, a little more cowboy and more accepted by the crew. Sometime in the late fifties or early sixties Bobby got put on the Allan-Herschell merry-go-round, and he found a home. His second man for a time was Paul Haugland from Belmond, Iowa. More will be said about Paul later as he went on to become a key person in the organization and own rides of his own. On the merry-go-round, Arbuckle's organizational skills quickly developed.

Arbuckle was definitely a "point and direct" kind of a foreman. He knew that the better crew he had, the less he would actually have to lift and carry himself. That is no adverse criticism. The object in setting up or tearing down is to have stuff properly lifted and carried and not who is doing the lifting and carrying. If it was a three- day week-end spot and set up was on Friday morning, Bobby would start recruiting his teardown crew from among the locals on Friday afternoon and have them check in periodically over the next couple of days so they were sure to be there for Sunday night. He would start the truck a couple of times during the spot and especially in the early afternoon the last day just to be sure there were no problems with the battery. He wanted to be ready. If the show closed by 10:30 and he could have a two- hour teardown the local beer joint stayed open 'till one. By this time, having been in town a few days, Bob knew the bartender's first name and, probably, the names of his children and dog. For the most part, the beer drinking didn't start until the 1948 Allan-Herschell merry-go-round was safely and properly loaded in the truck and ready to be driven to the next spot. Once- in a while Bob would get inconveniently drunk before teardown and a "sub" would have to be called in off the bench. A few times the "sub" was Mitchell Buxton – a longtime concession owner from Austin, Minnesota. In this sense, a carnival is like a football team. If tearing down is like being in the game, and the coach says, "Buxton, go in for Arbuckle!" there is no question. Buxton heaves a big sigh, rounds up his entire crew and "goes in for Arbuckle". The merry-go-round gets loaded in the truck.

As testimony to Bob's delegating ability, when he was a pall bearer at Al Merriam's funeral in Ogden, Iowa, Dale commented, "That was the only time he had actually seen Bobby carry anything.

Cleaning rags or "grease rags" were also high on Bobby's priority. If anyone wanted or needed a rag to wipe up an oil spill or clean a ride seat Arbuckle had them. One of the first things Bobby would do after arriving in a new spot was send local kids to raid their mother's closets, dresser drawers and rag bags for "grease rags". At the regular repeat dates, often times, the local kids would meet his truck as he came into town eager to exchange their bags of carefully saved rags for free ride tickets. The office had no problem giving the complimentary tickets to Bobby. He was providing a valuable service to the whole show.

Robert Arbuckle probably didn't have as many wives over the years as it seems, but he had several. From the period of 1953 till 2003 there were at least four or five and maybe more. Some were on the show with him, and some were not. He was a ladie's man in his own unique way. When he got "duded up" in his cowboy garb he looked as if he had just stepped off the cover of a nineteen-fifties Ernest Tubb record album. He could have been one of the Texas Troubadours themselves. A western shirt with pearl snap buttons, polished black boots, black hat and a wide western belt with two buckles, one on either side of his whip thin and flat belly gave Bobby a dashing if, somewhat, honky-tonk look.

The season of 1993 was interesting toward the end as it involved two of Bobby's wives, a stabbing and a demonstration of his resourcefulness and being able to think on his cowboy booted feet. Bobby was living in the merry-go-round van with wife no. n (where n is an integer from 3 to 6). Like many marriages where sometimes the relationship get a little rocky Bob and wife n were having a dispute. By the time the show got to the Martin County Fair in Fairmont, Minnesota things proceeded beyond rocky, and she stabbed Bobby in the chest with a knife he happened to have in their bunk. The wound, though not fatal, required hospitalization and her to leave town. Bobby was not released from the hospital until after the spot was over and the show had moved to Fergus Falls. The route was Fergus Falls, MN, Brookings, SD, Winner, SD, Pierre, SD, and long-time traditional closing spot of the season, the Corn Palace Celebration in Mitchell, SD. Bobby's dilemma was several fold, namely, he was almost broke, had no place to live, no transportation and needed a little more convalescing before he could go back to work. And then, as he related, later on, almost as if by divine vision, he remembered he had an ex-wife in Mountain Lake, Minnesota a short 45 miles away. With a phone call and a few words of explanation and he was in her car heading for Mountain Lake and a couple of weeks of R and R. There being no point chasing the show around playing 3 and 4 day spots when he could meet the show in Mitchell which was a ten day event and retrieve his job and season end bonus. It never occurred to him that both job and bonus would not be there for him. The ex-wife delivered him to 2nd and Main in Mitchell and once again he was on his own. The show wouldn't arrive for a few days. Bobby counted his meager bankroll, assessed the situation, walked a half a block south to the Longhorn Bar, greeted the bartender by name and proceeded to get roaring drunk.

At first his actions appear total irresponsible and that he is incapable of looking out for himself. Arbuckle knew several things that might not occur to the average guy. First he didn't have enough money to rent a motel room, buy food for several days, or obtain transportation to where ever the show was. Further- more, in a few days the show would be in Mitchell and he would be back with his friends, his job, his "house" and his season end bonus. He also knew something a less worldly person would most likely not know. What he knew was that Mitchell, South Dakota had a very well run and active alcohol rehabilitation facility run by the City of Mitchell and the Police Department. It was located right down town and only one- half block from where the carnival would be setting up in a few days.

The plan worked to perfection. When the show arrived the local police informed Dale, who was running the show by this time, that Bobby was in rehab and would he please go get him. When Dale went to rehab there was Bobby. He had had a clean bed each night, a fresh shower, three meals a day, wearing clean clothes from the Salvation Army and was playing a rousing game of checkers with one of his fellow boarder. When the show opened on September 16, 1993 Bobby was at his assigned post ready for riders. The horses and the chrome upon which they are suspended we brightly polished as were Arbuckle's black boots, and he was back in the saddle again.

He died in the spring of 2003 in Jefferson Iowa having come north with the show. As a way of remembering him, on the day of his funeral one horse was turned around backward on the merry-go-round and no one was allowed to ride it. The show was in Centerville, Iowa, and many friends and show people attended the funeral.

Stanley Rupp, Belle Plaine, Iowa

Stan Rupp appeared on the scene during the Missing Decade when Dale was not on the show. Stanley came from a large family who lived in the small eastern Iowa town of Belle Plaine. Belle Plaine lies about twenty-five miles east of Tama, and, has a population of just over 2,500. It is quite understandable that Tama and the surrounding area would be rich for the requiting of help given the number of times the show played there. As of this writing the early May date in Tama – sponsored by the Fire Department - is the longest, continuously "played" date on Merriam's route. Some dates were played earlier, such as Winona Steam Boat days, but there were years during this time when Winona choose a different carnival thus, the years were not continuous. This would have been during the Arbuckle era but after the "Johnny, Ronnie and Frank period. Stan's arrival would have been in the mid-sixties – a period that could be called the Paul Haugland, Arbuckle, Kenny Spurgeon era.

Stan had a clean shaven, blond hair, and a swagger that made him likeable and un-likeable at the same time. It's unknown how he learned the Tilt-A-Whirl, but learn it he did. Leo Stuker must have been his second man and would have had some knowledge buried back in that thick skull of his. Leo was everyone's second man for a period of about ten years or more. Stan had the energy and general cockiness to be a tilt foreman if he was, perhaps, a little rough on the extra help. A typical work directive on teardown night might be, "Come on sparrow-arms, grab that steel!" Or, to speed up the operation, "Get that blocking, my grandma's slow, but she's old. What's your excuse"? The usual amount of swearing and foul language took place, but somehow, out of Stan's mouth, it was just –well- Stan.

Unfortunately, early in his time as a ride boy, he was badly injured in an automobile accident that took him out of the picture for a couple of years, or more. His friends and fellow ride boys, like Paul Haugland, who knew him before and after say that he was never as strong, and, even not a big as before the accident. His spirit was still there, however, and he could still "move that steel" and get "sparrow-armed" extra help to work right along- side him. He and Arbuckle shared that trait. They knew the job to be done whether it was tearing down, operating a ride on a busy afternoon in the sun, or setting up had to be done. They could recruit local extra help and then work with what help was available. They were going to have their beer that night, and the sooner the work was done the sooner the beer could be drunk (and so could they be – drunk, that is).

Stan Rupp and Robert Arbuckle died within days of each other, and some show members attended both funerals during the week the show played the Firemen's Celebration in Centerville, Iowa.

Others

Another north central Iowa town with a population of 2000 to 2500 supplied a disproportional number of ride boys during the late sixties and early seventies. That was Belmond – a long time date on the show's route. Sponsored by the Jaycees and later by the city parks and rec. department it offered a Monday – Wednesday date in early June when the show was into its "two-a-week" spring fling.

Paul Haugland

Principal among these (and the source of this list) was Paul Haugland. Paul's years were 1966 through 1973 and then again in 1982 when the show got its first Zipper and was under Dale's watch and leadership. Big, red headed, good natured, and eager to learn the business, Paul easily and quickly made friends with rideboys, game people and the Merriam family. His first job was as second man on the Merry-go-round under Arbuckle. His first truck to drive on a jump was not a truck at all but the boss's Cadillac pulling the eighteen- foot office trailer. Edna drove the house with a Chevrolet pick-up (remember the rule – the woman drove the house) following Al in a truck and Paul with the office bring up the rear of the three- vehicle convoy. Paul quickly moved on the becoming the Eli Scrambler foreman. He and Bruce Carlson from Ogden became good friends and between the two of them learned to do almost every job on the show, especially where rides, trucks or generators were concerned. In 1973-74 Paul bought a Rock-O-Plane, Loop-O-Plane, and a funhouse and booked them as independent rides for a number of years. With a true love for the industry, Paul supplied a number of ideas, pictures and names for the completion of this book.

The Belmond Ride Boys

Paul Haugland (1966 – 1973, 1982)

Leland (PeeWee) Stoffer (1969, 1970, 1972) Worked on the Wheel and kid rides and the Trabant in 1972. he is in a nursing home in Florida -0 victim of a hit and run accident.

Lonnie Stoffer (1971) Worked on the Scrambler with Bruce Carlson. Lonnie committed suicide in 2001.

Tom (T J) Jenison (1970 – 1973, 198?) TJ worked on the Slide in 1970, the tilt in 1971 – 1973 and for one season he was Dale's truck maintenance man in the early nineties. TJ was loud, rough, and a heavy smoker. He would walk out of a parts store and go elsewhere if he wasn't permitted to smoke while doing business at the parts counter. Toward the end it was pretty obvious he was smoking more than just store- bought tobacco. During his last year Dale sent TJ to Minnesota Truck Inspection Certification School so that could do the state inspections on the trucks. A big help to the show at a time when the inspections were a new and troublesome thing.

Jon Elphic (1969 – 1971) Jon worked under Hubert Heeron on the wheel and two umbrella rides.

Randy Covington (1970 – 1971?) With Paul as a mentor, Randy worked on and Wheel and Scambler in 1970 – 1931.

Gene Theyer (1972) Tilt-A-Whirl died of cancer in 2008.

Ronnie Zwald (1959 – 196?)

Ronnie Zwald was from Ogden, and had know about the Merriam's Shows from the time he was very young. In 1959 he was sixteen, school was out and Ron visited the show in two early Iowa spring spots – Perry and Denison. Walter Lee (Shorty) was on the tilt that year, and somehow, he and Ronnie got acquainted. Ronnie claims Shorty put in a good word for him with Al. Whatever happened, Ronnie was hired at a salary of $45 per week and joined the show in Odebolt – a three- day street celebration where the show set up on Main Street. Ronnie's first job was on the wheel, and Dale was to teach him how to operate the ride. Only one wheel was set up in Odebolt, and the first afternoon was very slow. After a few jerky starts and stops Ron developed a feel for the clutch and brake fairly quickly. Now Ron must master the art of keeping the loaded wheel in balance. If one side of the wheel is heavier than the opposite one the ride is uneven or jerky. If the unbalance is extreme the motor may not be able to pull the heavy side over the top, at all. Starting with an empty wheel, typically seat no. 1 is loaded first, then seat no. 7, then 8, and then2 and 3. If no one else is in the ticket line the operator would run the ride with five loaded seats and only one seat out of balance. At the conclusion of the ride (about 1 ½ to 2 minutes, not counting loading time) the process is reversed – seat No. 3 would be unloaded first, then 2, then 7 and 8 and finally 1. This assumes no customers are waiting to get on the ride. If there are, of course, the operator wants to reload seats as passengers get off. What if the number waiting to ride differs from the ones getting off? Now the process becomes a little more complex. This is where Dale helped out the new operator, Ron.

Dale was, for some reason, selling tickets on the wheel that particular afternoon. In 1959 each ride had its own ticket box and ticket seller. The ticket booth (box) sat directly in front of the ride. A customer could buy his or her ticket, take a step or two to one side and be in the line to get on the ride. With the back door of the ticket box open Dale and Ron could easily talk to each other, and Dale could see which seats were loaded on the wheel. When the loading/unloading process began, Dale would look at the waiting line and call out the seat number to be unloaded and reloaded, thus keeping the wheel in balance. By the end of the afternoon Ronnie had figured out the pattern and was on his own. In an email, 53 years later, Ron shared this memory with Dale and reminded Dale of a certain local Odebolt girl, named Sharon, who was hanging around the ticket box that afternoon. Dale was a busy guy.

Ronnie Zwald married a young lady on the show, Janice Henderson. Janice's parents were Marvin and Evelyn Henderson of Park Rapids, Minnesota. They also had a son, Gene, who was just a few years younger than Janice. The Henderson's had the diggers on the show for twenty years, and were a classy family, to say the least. The Zwalds moved to Louisville, Kentucky, and along with Gene Henderson have supplied a large amount of invaluable information about rideboys of the sixtie's era.

James Arthur (Cotton) DeVaughn (1957? – 1965)

"Cotton" was unique in many ways and yet a typical rideboy. he and Dale good friends almost in the sense of a cowboy and his sidekick – but it wasn't always clear who was the sidekick and who was the cowboy. Cotton liked to play a question and answer game he called "general knowledge". Driving down the highway he might ask, "What is the state flower of Texas?" or "What is the capitol of Missouri?" He was playing trivia before it was popular. He worked on the tilt some, but he was just a little too gentle for that ride. He knew the ride, but it just wasn't a good fit. He worked on the coaster some and on the King Frolic. He was good around winter quarters, a good semi driver, and thought of himself as something of a midway poet. Cotton worked one season in Cundiff's cookhouse, and then came back to the rides.

Jerry Leeper

Jerry and Cotton were a two- man pact reminiscent of the Ronnie, Johnny and Frank, three-man pact of a few years before. Jerry was a "tilt man's tilt man" – smallish, but muscular and extremely well- coordinated. When he ran the Tilt-A-Whirl, he liked to jump on the moving platform (called the intermediate) and ride around on the ride standing up. He could move from one platform to the next section by dancing between the spinning tubs (seats) always planting his highly polished engineer boot on the next intermediate as if they were magnetic. This performance was usually much to the delight of young girl riders, and much to the displeasure of Al when he saw it. Jerry and his second man, Leo Stuker (Leo hung in there for a long time) along with two extra help could cheerfully tear the tilt down in about two hours, but there were no wasted motions. If a break was taken it was taken by all. No one smoked except when Jerry said it was time for a smoke break. If you were carrying a part, you carried it quickly. If you going to where a part was you ran – no slow walking allowed.

One of the last seasons Jerry was out he was the electrician. On teardown night it was the electrician's job to disconnect all the junction boxes and distribution wire and load them in the transformer truck. By necessity, this job was one of the last to be done on teardown night – electricity being needed almost to the end. This was circa 1960 before the show had its own generators. The transformer truck (hot wagon) was a portable power distribution station that would be connected to the local power system at each spot. That year Jerry was dating one of the girl show girls, and a wedding was held on the Platte County Fairgrounds in Columbus, Nebraska *(Seems like a lot of things happened in Columbus, including one of the first girls I ever kissed was behind Chief Little Wolf's girl show in Columbus, but that story will be told later)*. The ceremony took place in the girl show top before opening on Friday afternoon, the last day of the fair. All show personnel were invited, the bride's boss gave her away, local clergy conducted the service, and a cake and punch reception followed. Al made a few remarks in the form of a toast and announced that as a wedding gift, volunteers had been recruited to roll and load the wire that night. After some of his preliminary teardown jobs were done, the new groom could go to bed early. It was an overnight jump to Schuyler the next day opening Saturday at 6:00 PM so the honeymoon would be cut a bit short.

CHAPTER VII

THE JOINTEES

Carnivals have rides, shows, food concessions and, of course, games. Perhaps, if a cartoon were to be drawn of a carnival, after the Ferris wheel and merry-go-round were drawn, the cartoonist would turn his attention to the game operator drawn with a bow tie, a flat straw hat, sleeve garters and a caption offering a kewpie doll to the lucky customer who could knock all three milk bottles down with one ball. More often than not, the customer (less politically correct term might be a "mark" or "sucker") would look over his shoulder at his attentive girlfriend with an approval seeking plea in his eye, wind up with great flair and throw with all his might. The girlfriend would squeal, the gathered crowd would moan, and one or two of the bottles would fly off the stand and crash into the tin back drop with a satisfying bang.

"Sorry, friend, you have to get all three bottles down with one ball." "Give me another quarter (or half-dollar, or dollar, or two dollars – depending in what decade the scene was taking place) and win one for the little lady." Again, one or two bottles might be left standing. All those fancy hotels in Las Vegas weren't built by the winners. But, before long a persistent player with a good arm will wind up with a happy girlfriend on that arm as she gives her new teddy bear its first adoring hug.

Carnival games have come and gone, evolved and faded into extinction, and risen and declined in popularity during the seventy-five years of Merriam's history, but the one-ball is still with us. Longevity often breeds legend, and so it is with the one-ball. Consider the carnival "playing a spot" in, say, Wheatfield, Kansas. A tornado, a real Kansas twister, swept through the town and surrounding area. Barns, houses, churches and trees were leveled by the dozens. People evacuated the Wheatfield fairgrounds in droves via car, buggy and horseback. The carnival, exposed and vulnerable to the elements, suffered considerable damage. Tents were down, ticket booths were turned over, the Ferris wheel was leaning but upright thanks to the heroic efforts of the rideboys who tied it to truck frames, trees and other places of secure anchorage. When the storm had passed the clean- up began with each of the crew going to their work place to see what could be salvaged. Almost all of the twenty-odd game concessions (the joints) were flattened to the Kansas sod if they were to be found at all. Quietly and carefully Edward "One-ball Eddie" Jones gathered up the wet and torn canvas of his game, the teddy bears with missing eyes, ears and limbs, and two of the three milk bottles from the game, placing them carefully in the slough box. Turning, he reached for the third bottle. He had no trouble locating it amongst the wreckage and debris. He knew where it would be. He could have found it blindfolded in the dark. It was still standing on the game pedestal, perfectly up-right, disturbed by neither tempest nor thrown baseball, exactly where he had placed it to await the next player.

In As with the rideboys an organizational structure governs the games, their owners and the agents who operate them. Merriam's, for the most part, never owned any of the games on the show. The exceptions were when Dale was in high-school and had his own game and years later after the show had passed into his hands. This arrangement, where the show owned the rides and held the primary contract for the fair or event, was pretty much followed industry wide post world war II. There were exceptions, of course, but, for the most part, the carnival owner owned the rides, and supplied water, power and other life necessities, made the rules, and sub-contracted the games, food concessions, side shows, and even extra rides. This contractor - sub-contractor relationship created a layer within a layer- in the carnival organization. A game owner may own and book with the carnival two, three, maybe a dozen or more games. The game owner needs the carnival because the show has the contract and the exclusive, legal right to set up and operate at a particular fair or event. The reciprocal need is that the carnival needs games to round out the midway, have enough entertainment for the attending crowds, the income provided by the rent or privilege fee the game owner pays to the carnival.

In more recent years this fee or privilege has come to be called by the somewhat polite and politically correct term, "rent". The rent might be calculated by the "front foot". If a game takes 25 feet of linear space on the midway and the show charges $25 per foot then the rent would be $625, and that is the amount the game owner would pay to the show for the privilege of operating at that spot. On Merriam's it was more common for the concessions, both games and food to pay a flat, set fee for the rent regardless of the space required on the midway. The third way of determining the rent was as a percentage of gross sales. This was more common for food concessions and games of chance that paid off in cash (when local laws and/or the constabulary permitted) instead of merchandise. However, assessed and paid, the rent provided an income stream for the show.

Just as some color fades from old paintings also, some color is fading from the language of the carnival. To an old-timer the term is not rent. Rent is something you pay to stay in a room over the barber shop while the show is town. Rent is something you do to a Hertz car at the airport. If you book three joints with Windy Van Hooten's Wonder Shows in West Overshoe, Texas you pay Windy the "nut". The fee you pay is not rent nor privilege – it's the "nut". The term, "a tough nut to crack" might be used to refer to an initial fee or charge that appears to be excessively high initially and difficult to overcome. The term "nut", folklore has it, has nothing at all to do with the fruit of a walnut tree, nor any other tree for that matter. It refers to the nut that screws onto the end of threaded shaft to secure something to that shaft. Consider a time when carnival games moved from town to town in wagons. Machine tools were not as standardized as they are today. The nuts that secured the wagon wheels to their appointed axels were individually machined and not interchangeable with the other three wheels or with some other wagon down the street. If you lost an axel nut you had to have the local blacksmith or machine shop custom make a replacement nut before you could continue on any intended journey. The carnival owner of old could pretty much insure a game owner would pay his rent before leaving town by removing and keeping one of the game owner's wheel NUTS. When the rent was paid the nut was returned and both parties had fulfilled their contractual obligation. Thus, "pay to get your nut back". "pay the nut".

Before world war II Merriam's typically did not book any games. Al and Edna booked their rides as independents. If they coexisted at a fair or celebration with other games, shows or rides each entity was booked with the event sponsor (the committee) on their own. This arrangement led to great networking opportunities and this molecular-like movement of rides games, food concessions, and shows allowed friendships and business relationships to develop. One such friendship was between Al Merriam and Bob Robinson of Mason City, Iowa.

In the first half of the twentieth- century it was not just the kids that played carnival games

Many games catered to Mom and Dad and to Grandpa and Grandma, too. There were grocery wheels where the prizes offered were household items. Hams, liquor, baskets of fruit, blankets and lamps were all featured. The men played gambling games, called "pc" or "percentage" because they usually paid their nut as a percentage of the winnings, and the women played bingo. Of the games that appealed to the grown-ups BINGO was the unchallenged king. It was housed in the biggest top. It gave out during the season virtual semi-truck loads of lamps, card tables, Beacon blankets, and mirrors of all kinds. Most carnivals carried at least one, if not two or three bingos, but if Windy Van Hooten had any in West Overshoe he would have a "corn game" and not a "bingo". It would use bingo game cards with letters B, I , N, G, and O across the top and twenty-four numbered squares filling the card. A random arrangement of five numbers one through fifteen under the B, sixteen though thirty under the I and so on. When counter men had sold all the cards they could the caller would begin the game with his best radio announcer-like voice and say, "All right, ladies and gentlemen, please place a kernel of corn in the center of your card marked free." "Your first number is under the I... twenty- three. I ... twenty-three".

Big, golden kernels of Midwest field corn were used for the markers. Those kernels must have had a familiar feel as the Midwest farm wife carefully placed the fifth one in a row, column, or diagonal and boldly called out, "Bingo". The corn game dominated the midway in those mid-century days both in size and player popularity. Some bingo operators went on to become show owners themselves while other show owners took ownership positions in the corn games on their shows as a lucrative business investment. Bob Robinson, L.O. Weaver, and Art B. Thomas would be examples.

If corn games dominated the midway Bob Robinson's corn games would dominate in the upper Midwest of Iowa and southern Minnesota. They were magnificent in size, flash and the display of prizes offered. Beacon blankets were the featured item hanging from the tent's two-by-four rafters and making a colorful tapestry like ceiling lighted by the glow of the 150- watt yellow light bulbs that dangled from the two-conductor twisted brewery cord light stringer. With Robinson's bingo the winner always got choice of any prize in the game. No coupons to save, small prizes to trade for bigger prizes, the winner always got choice. In case of a tie numbers were drawn from a cigar box with the high number getting choice and the low number receiving a free game.

Bob Robinson and his wife Irene were from Mason City in north central Iowa from where they had operated a successful game business for a number of years. Although they featured their bingo's they also offered scales, pan games, ball games, dart games, etc. and had accumulated a wide network of acquaintances in the business. During the partnership years (1947 – 1948) Robinson handled all the games, food concessions and side shows.

Anson White: Stopped to say hello in Waterloo during My Waterloo Days in 2009. He worked for Bob Robinson in 1947 and 1948 in the corn game- on Merriam and Robinson Shows. When that partnership dissolved, he stayed with Robinson – off and on – with the new Robinson's Greater Shows. He talked about playing Britt (Iowa) Hobo Days and what a big spot it was. Merriam and Robinson played it in '47 and '48, but when the partnership split the spot went to Robinson.

White also ran the scale joint (guess your age or weight). We talked abou, how the agent would write his guess on a pad of note paper – usually a white three by five pad - and then ask the player (customer – "mark") how old they were or checked their weight on a scale. The player won if the guesser failed to guess within three pounds or two years. Then the agent, (guesser) would, with noticeable flourish, tear off the sheet of note paper and throw it on the ground. Littering was much less of a concern in 1947 as was political correctness. By the end of a three-day spot the ground around a good scale agent's joint was evidence of how much business was done and, in a way, part of the gaff to the joint.

The scale joint is one that has faded from midways of the twenty-first century. When they were at the height of their popularity the prizes were usually cast plaster dolls, gaily painted and overlaid with sparkles. Some operators made their own "plaster", as the item was called, by copying the more popular items purchased from the stock companies such as Acme or Wisconsin Deluxe. This was accomplished by repeatedly dipping the pattern piece in liquid rubber to make a thin rubber mold of the original. Plaster of Paris was purchased at the local drug store and bright colors of paint from the hardware or "dime store. Thus, through the somewhat labor- intensive process of dipping, pealing, mixing, painting, and applying glitter a pretty good copy could be ready to be offered as a prize for less than the 35 to 50 cents purchase price. Though carnival plaster isn't used for prizes anymore it has become a sought- after collector's item.

The Campbells

Lawrence (Larry) Campbell was the last scale agent to be around Merriam's. Lawrence was the son of Bill and Helen Campbell from Deloit, Iowa and was on the show from the mid-fifties to the early sixties. They operated two straight sales concessions – Bill sold tricks and novelties out of a trailer-type concession with one opening side awning while Helen sold and engraved souvenir jewelry from a separate stand. Helen's stand was technically a knockdown jewelry spindle. It was a knockdown because it could be taken apart and loaded into another vehicle, and a jewelry spindle because as well as straight sale items, customer could pay a set price and win an item by spinning the big wooden arrow in the center of the front counter. The item "won" could then be engraved with initials, name, date, etc.

Bill's novelties were strictly straight sales. One interesting thing about Bill Campbell and the way he ran his novelties was his phenomenal memory. This allowed him to not have to have the prices marked on any of his merchandize He had to interact with each and every customer. They had to ask the price of anything about which they were interested. The fact is, Bill's memory was not as good as he thought. Sometimes, a shy ten year old girl, who obviously only had the one quarter she tightly held in her tiny hand, found out the price of the bright red baton cane she looked at so longingly was exactly 25 cents. Bill had forgotten only ten minutes before that the price of that baton cane was really a dollar, and was purchased by a young man headed for the dance with his sweetheart on his arm. Bill's memory also failed him when he displayed his merchandize. He always had a few items under the back shelf, but their location and price could always be recalled if the right class of potential customer came by. In the present twenty-first century these items would be right out there beside the red baton, but the mid-fifties were a gentler time.

The Campbells lived (on the road that is – they had a house in Deloit) in a camper that mounted on the back of a pick-up. This let them pull the novelty trailer behind and load the jewelry joint in the novelty trailer. Lawrence was attending the University of Northern Iowa, and played a few short seasons. He later taught and was a principal in Tucson.

Russell Frey

Of all the game owners and agents during the first 20 years of Merriam's Midway Shows, Russell Frey was surely the most unique. Russell came from a family of five boys and one girl in West Union, Iowa – population about 2000 in the northeast corner of the state. West Union is the home of the popular Fayette County Fair, and the Frey family would certainly attend each August. Somehow, Russell was attracted to the carnival midway, as his niece, Phyllis Frey, relates the story, and got a job as the "roughy" for one of the game operators. A "roughy" was hired to do the various menial tasks for the game agent, such as, drive stakes, open and close the awnings, clean the counters and carry stock. A travelling roughy set up and tore down the game, as well. Whether Russell was travelling yet or not is not known, but one afternoon, before the midway was open, Russell had the awning part way open making things ready when an interested, potential customer poked his head under the awning and asked, "What do you do here?" Russell had watched how the game was played. This was his chance. He had his "mark". They played a few games. Russell took his money, and later turned it over to the game operator. The regular agent was impressed with young Russell's performance, allowed him to work as an agent a few more times and a career was launched.

The Freys were related to the Merriams remotely through Alva's mother's side of the family, but that remote relationship never seemed to come into play as far as Russell's position on the Show. Russell was single (as in never married), conspicuously neat, clean, and a snappy dresser. During the fifties and sixtie's the people working on the midway did so in their own clothes – no uniforms or show shirts were issued or required. Russell's outfits were always unique and a little more flashy than anyone else's on the lot. His dress and the fact that he reeked of Old Spice after shave lotion was his bally – standing straight to his full 5' 6" height in the center of his joint, dressed neatly in what would be called now "resort casual", and using all of the customer's senses (including smell) as they walked by.

During the fifties Russell operated only one game. It was a roll-down, and, could be loaded into a Chevrolet panel truck which in turn pulled his house trailer. Russell's trailer was the smallest on the lot. Again, he was neat, clean and self- contained. His game was a "roll- down" or "Over and Under". The player would roll ten small rubber balls (one at a time) down an inclined wooden table into chutes numbered 1 through 5. The player would win if their total score was <u>under</u> 17 or <u>over</u> 37. The prize was a nice, big, cuddly teddy bear. Except for color, all the prizes displayed in the joint were the same. If you won, you got a teddy bear. With the combination of Russell's soft- spoken charm, his good looks and the cloud of Old Spice, every girl on the lot between ten and twenty just had to have one of those bears. His act was almost always the same and never seemed to get old. When a player would win Russell would put on a show of absolute joy that they had won a prize. Then just as he was handing out the bear he would draw back slightly with a pained smile and say, with much over-acting, "O, I hate it when the girls win one of these bears. They hug'em so and I get so jealous I just can't stand it!". Then he would give the lucky girl the bear and again go into his act.

"Oh! Oh! Look at that! She's going to hug it! Oh! Oh!"

Now, during this bear hugging act he has started at least two more games if there are players – making change for a twenty if necessary and keeping the bills faced. What Russell could not do well was count and add numbers as he flipped the rubber balls out of the numbered chutes to determine if the player had won. The faster he would flip the balls and count, his accuracy may or may not improve. For example, the first time a player played the game it seemed he or she would miss winning by one or two points – say a score of 19 or 35. After a few more players gathered around, and it looked as if it would be a good time for a winner, that player would get good enough at the game to hit 15 or 16 – a winner. With the bear hugging routine going on, and a teenage girl jumping up and down screaming, no one noticed or bothered to say anything if they had noticed that two 3's and a 5 didn't add up to 9 as Russell had counted. By that time two more games had started, and the money was in game's change apron. Russell never claimed he could count good, but he smelled great.

Russell left the show for a few years in the fifties to try his skills in Las Vegas. Those must have been great days in the classic Vegas just before the "Rat Pack" years. He was a crap dealer at the Golden Nugget in downtown Vegas. Teenaged Dale was an eager listener to those tales and yarns and soaked up those stories like that Iowa soil could soak up a two- inch rain.

Russell was also very innovative and made considerable contributions to the carnival game industry. He was very much involved, if not solely responsible for the evolution of the Crazy Ball game. That game became so popular that stock companies like Wisconsin Deluxe, Acme and Oriental Trading Company (known in the business as "the Jap"), developed a line of stuffed animals specifically for that game. A variety of merchandise was "born" to be forever known as "Crazy Ball Stock".

As every innovation and new idea has roots and beginnings, the beginning of the Crazy Ball game was in the Pan Game. The "Pan Game" name came from the playing board, or table, which consisted of a rectangle of muffin tins attached to a table top approximately 4 feet by 5 feet. The "cups" in the tins were painted different colors. The number of different colors depended on the design of that particular game. The one Dale and Alicia owned in the early eighties was a four- color game. It was quick, easy to run and very popular. The parameter of the table was contained by a fence-like boundary of light door springs. The players would place or "bet" money on the color of their choice on the counter boards on one of the three side of the game booth. A soft rubber ball was tossed by one of the players onto the table which after a few bounces around the table would land in a colored cup. The player on that color would receive cash back at the odds for that color. The other players on non-winning colors forfeited their money and the next game would begin. It was a popular, fun, adult game, and profitable for the show and the game operators. The problem was that it was gambling, pure and simple, and illegal in most states.

What made it gambling, in the eyes of many law enforcement officials was the fact that it "payed off" in cash. Russell thought he could keep the popular game legally operating if he used something other than cash for the pay off. Remember that this was the late fifties and cigarettes were advertised, popular and many people smoked. A pack of cigarettes cost about 50 cents. Russell kept the pan game concept and paid off in cigarettes. The pan game was now the "Cigarette Game". The midway, had a whole new game, and a new bally joined the cacophony

"Play a dime and win a pack. Play a quarter win two packs, play two packs win a carton". Most popular brands were kept in stock, and the game quickly became a midway favorite. Once again, however, social forces came to bear. For one thing the game could only be played by those over the age of eighteen (twenty-one in some areas). Payment of the retail tobacco tax was an issue. And, even in the fifties and sixties, there was the beginning of a stigma against smoking.

Russell's answer to these critics was to change the cigarette game to the new "Gum Chum". Surely no one could object to something as innocent as chewing gum except, perhaps, an overly cranky school teacher, and, anyway it was summer, and school was out. Gum could be purchased wholesale in six-pack cartons, or "bundles" of gum. The word "bundles" seemed convenient to avoid any confusion with cigarettes. The bally was now, "Come in chum and win some gum. Play a quarter (it might have been a dime in the beginning) win a bundle of gum." The operator would make a big deal out of "calling the game as the ball rolled and bounced on the table, "Who's the winner? Who shot it? Who's got it? Is it red? Is it black? How do you do? It looks like blue. The winner is blue, BLU blue." The winning color was always spelled out in three letter abbreviations. Black was "BLK, black", green was "GRN, green", and so forth. Red was a bit of a problem, and was, simply and boringly, "RED, red".

The game was well run, presented no problems with the local law enforcement, and popular – kind of. Winning gum just didn't generate the type of excitement necessary for a really good game. Something needed to be tweaked. Russell found some smaller teddy bears which closely resembled the ones used in other games but were less expensive. They were cute, cuddly and just as "huggable" as the larger variety, and might just work in the Gum Chum. Now the play could parlay his/her winnings into something more fun than a bundle of chewing gum. They still won gum, but now could play bundles of gum back and win a small teddy bear. It wasn't long before the game morphed again allowed the player to play back a small bear and win a larger, full sized bear in its place.

The next step in the evolution is obvious. Eliminate the gum.

"Choose your color – join right in – it's only a quarter – you can win". The colors were still spelled out in three letters – "The winner is green, GRN, green", but the "rafters" were filled with colorful stuffed animals (plush), and a funnel like net was suspended over a spinning multi-colored, horizontal wheel into which the ball was tossed. The birth and evolution of the Crazy Ball was complete, and every step could be witnessed on Merriam's Midway Shows.

Russell left Merriam's sometime in the early sixties and toured with the Ray Drescher Shows in Minnesota. There was no apparent problem with Merriam's – maybe he just wanted a change. Russell's brother Marty Frey came over with an arcade and a pc game called a "block joint". Dale and Alicia both worked in the block joint briefly while visiting the show during vacations. Later- on, Marty bought the Henderson's digger operation on the show and had penny falls (called "nudgers") into the early eighties.

Russell Frey died March 11, 1976 at age 60 at his winter quarters in Harlingen, Texas. He was murdered by two armed men who came to rob him and did.

The Single O's

In the fifties and sixties it wasn't uncommon for a couple (or even a family) to own and operate just one game. After about 1970, the business, the economy, the expenses all changed, and the single game-single owner/operator just wasn't practical. Another changing factor was that the number of games featured on the midway became less. In 1974, the first season under Dale and Alicia's ownership, they presented 25 "joints", in Cannon

Falls, Minnesota at the Cannon Valley Fair. In the early to mid -fifties that number was about forty and as high as 45. The general growth of the fair was just the opposite. The ride gross sales were up, the general attendance was up. The good game operators recognized the change and survived, the others did not.

CHAPTER VIII

THE GALS, LADIES AND
TOUGH TITTED BROADS

There is little question that owning, working on and moving a traveling carnival is a man's world and life style. Having said and accepted that premise, examples of strong, interesting and dominate women leap from the pages of carnival history. The history of Merriam's Midway Shows is no exception. There is no way to rank the "ladies of the show" in any kind of order of importance, interest, or influence. Even listing them chronologically fails because of overlapping times on the show, changing jobs, and changing husbands/boyfriends, for that matter. What has been done here is to write a number of brief biographies of memorable women on the show trying to capture their personalities, quirks and strengths and go to print without regard to any particular order. The reader is free to rank them in any way he wishes according to which attribute seems appropriate.

The three categories suggested by the chapter title would seem to be self- explanatory. If any further definition is required for the reader the biographies should clear things up. The ladies – and there were several – were ladies in the recognized sense of "ladies and gentlemen". Edna Merriam was a lady. Alicia Merriam, Robby Merriam, Rose Johnson were ladies. The "gals" were gals because they weren't guys. The reader will have to pick them out from the following biographies. Nancy Krueger - much more about her later – was with the show from 1975 until 2011 - a long career in any industry, to be sure. Nancy was probably the originator of the colorful and descriptive term – "tough titted broad". Nancy had a unique way of getting right to the truth of the matter, and the "ttb" was right on target.

Roger Kvern used a similar term, but probably because it was a man describing a woman, his phrase did not catch on as popular usage. There were a few seasons where Dale's daughter, Trissa, worked in the office behind the office window facing the outdoors, the midway and the world. The office girl (office manager) was the first contact anyone had wanting to do business with the carnival management. She paid the fuel man, the tire man, received the FEDEX and UPS shipments and could find the boss if the boss was really needed. She would also reimburse employees and staff for various expenses they might incur, such as, a gas receipt for Roger Kvern's pick-up because he drove to the next town to buy a tire for one of the ride trucks. Trissa was as frugal and tight with the company's money as Roger was loose. There was many a time when Trissa would go over Roger's receipts with an eye to examining every detail to make sure a pack of cigarettes or a cup of coffee didn't get charged to <u>Tools, Paint and Supplies.</u> Roger had great respect for Trissa, and really liked her. The evidence of that liking is his nickname for her. To Roger, Trissa was "Iron Bra".

For a while, during, the nineties, Nancy Krueger, Marion Nealon, and Judy Cummings would work some in the office. Marion dubbed them "Bitches Behind Glass". Let's meet the girls.

Nancy Krueger, of Austin Minnesota, has to lay claim to longevity. She and her Husband, Kenny, joined the show in the early 70's, when Dale purchased a fun house from Bucky Buxton, and since the tradition was, if the piece of equipment you worked on was sold, the new owner may well offer you the same job. Following that tradition, Kenny went to work for Dale. His wife, Nancy, went along with the deal. Her first job was selling tickets at Pine Island. Nancy tells the story of her first day at work, selling tickets in a wooden ticket box, in front of Dale's two wheels. He asked her if he could make change, she said, "yes", Dale said, "good, I'll get you a break in a little while". With that, Dale left, and Nancy didn't see a break for four hours. When her ticket box checked out, Dale must have thought, I found another gal. It wasn't many days before Nancy deserved the promotion to the next category. Nancy, and Kenny, both, went on to serve more than thirty years of devoted service to the show. Dale conducted funeral services for Nancy upon her death.

Marion Nealon had to be an all- time favorite Ferris wheel operator. Not everyone, and certainly very few gals, can operate a wheel, let alone, set up, tear down, and maintain the same, but, Marion could. Her talents were used on other rides as well. One time in Mason City, Dale was disappointed in his Kiddie ride crew, and how long it took them to set up the Hampton ride. Dale said, "Marion, and I could set up that ride in fifty- five minutes". Marion, knowing Dale was not one to make empty boasts, she knew she was in for it now. The stage was set. A lot stake was driven at its location on the lot. The Kiddie ride crew were told to sit in lawn chairs and witness the event. Walter Marson was the time keeper, and said, 'go'. Marion ran for the truck, started the engine, and made ready to back up. Dale, ran for the back of the truck, and loosened the chain binders. When the ride was on its location, and leveled, Dale and Marion assembled the track, and umbrella ride top, elapsed time of about thirty-five minutes. As the last of the five boats was attached, Dale threw the light switch, threw his hat in the air, and Walter, with a full show of authority, proclaimed, "fifty-three minutes". The Kiddie ride crew enjoyed the show. Dale breathed new life and spirit into his work crew, Marion gave a big sigh of relief, and took a break in the near by lawn chairs, and said, "boss, don't take me on any more dates". There is no doubt, Marion earned her rank in the female carnival hierarchy.

Judy Cummings was without a doubt, a blessing sent from a big midway in the sky. One day in Austin Minnesota, she just "showed up". She worked on the Marry-Go-Round first. Ernie, her traveling companion, was given work on the bumper cars. Judy had two valuable assets, she could sell tickets, and had a driver's license. These two talents would get you a job almost any day. To show Judy's toughness, when Dale first met her, she had made a home for Ernie and her, in the Merry-Go-Round light box. (Remember the Merry-Go-Round man on Sunset amusement). Judy quickly made friends with Nancy, and Marion, and The Boss. As the next thirty years rolled by, Judy sold tickets, drove various trucks, and advanced her way to an air- conditioned bunkhouse. Her value to the show was large indeed. Another example of her versatility, she was once sent on a double-back. When her truck wouldn't start, Judy suggested they try to jump-start, and she revealed she had taken the precaution of carrying jumper cables in her purse.

Now that's a Tough Titted Braud!!

Having made the above disclaimer regarding order, one particular lady and only one has to be first. Without her there would have been no Merriam's Midway Shows. Al Merriam might have met someone else and found himself in the carnival business. Edna certainly had no carnival roots, but then neither did Al. Would another young woman have had the patience and toughness to live in a tent, drive the car and house trailer with little sleep, sell tickets from an open top ticket booth with her young son asleep on the wooden seat beside her, and nurse Al though his bouts with migraine headaches? Maybe a carnival would have been born, but it would not have been Merriam's Midway Shows. Edna's influence is undeniable.

Edna Merriam (The beginning until 1986)

If anything, Edna was a lady. Born in 1910, tall (5'10") and lean (but big boned), the youngest of six farm family children she was not easily intimidated. For the time in which she lived she was always properly dressed. She put on a girdle and nylons with a skirt or dress every day.

Meet some others – with apologies to any left out and sincere thanks to those included.

Marion Nealon (The glory seasons of the nineties)

Clara Bollenbarger (The early fifties)

Clara and Luke Bollenbarger were from Aransas Pass, Texas and had the Six Cat game concession and probably one or two other games as well, but the Six Cat was their primary business. Luke was as typical an East Texan as God ever created. If a Hollywood director called central casting and asked for someone to play an East Texan Luke would be the man. Luke wasn't lazy, he just moved slow. He was willing enough, it was just that he avoided any body motion until the last possible moment. He talked slow and walked slow and that was all there was to it.

Clara on the other hand was whip thin, and gave the impression that she had a coiled spring inside her spine that might unleash into action at any time. They had a big, yellow straight truck with about an eighteen foot body that also pulled their house trailer. Clara drove the truck and Luke rode beside her from town to town. On teardown night one of the light hearted breaks one could take was watching Clara and Luke "hook up" the truck to the house trailer to be ready for the "jump" the next morning. Clara is the driver, of course, all one hundred pounds of her clinging to the steering wheel of that two-ton truck. This was 1950 without benefit of power steering. The power doing the steering was Clara power. Luke's job was to give her audible directions to allow her to guide the ball hitch of the truck directly under the coupler on the trailer so that a "hook up" could be made. Those listening and watching would hear, just as sure as if it were a scripted radio series, Luke slowly drawl out, "B r i n g I t b a c k a l I t t l e f u r t h e r, H o n e y".

To get an idea of the cadence try reading his words out loud, but make them consume a full fifteen seconds on your watch. As might be expected, the reaction time of Clara's left foot on the clutch pedal was quicker than her audible directions. A few times Clara would back up too far and bump the truck ball against the A-frame or the coupler of the trailer before Luke could say, "W h o a, H o n e y". No harm was done, and the only recourse was, "T a k e i t a h e a d a l I t t l e, H o n e y" Directions left and right were a little more complex, but somehow they were accomplished. After all, trailers are hooked up in East Texas every day.

Clara set up the joints, rolled the wire and water hose, tore down the joints, cooked the meal, and ran the house. Clara and Luke were on the show two or three season. About the second year, the show was playing the Kossuth County Fair in Algona, Iowa. Algona was always one of Al's favorite spots, and the show had about a fifty year history with the last year there being 1983. Clara drove into Algona that year in the fifties several months pregnant. Typically (and this year would have been no different) the jump was over night from Titonka Indian Days. Titonka was two days on the streets (Monday and Tuesday), which meant tear down Tuesday night, drive twenty-five miles to Algona, set up and open to a big, dime kid's day 1:00 PM Wednesday. Usually this was no problem except this year Clara had to make one additional stop. That was at the Algona hospital conveniently located east of the fairgrounds just across US No. 169. Clara stopped the truck, checked into the hospital, had the baby, stayed a night or two and drove the truck four days later to Sac City, Iowa.

CHAPTER IX

THE SHOWMEN – CHIEF LITTLE WOLF, JOHN – THE STONE MAN

A 21st century fairgoer might well look at the midway and the entertainment options it offers and wonder why the word "Shows" is often the last word in the name of that midway. Wouldn't "Rides, Games and Food Concessions" be more descriptive? Where are the shows as indicated in the title? A twentieth century fairgoer, especially one from the first half of that century, probably would not have that thought. During the industry's first 75 years, or so, shows were a very important part of a carnival's entertainment offering. There were girl shows, "At" shows, jig shows, mechanical shows, ten-in-one side shows and all sorts of single attraction shows like "pickled punks", frozen sharks, and, of course, the "Whatizit" show. The bally for this one was marvelous. "It's not a cat, not a rat, not a raccoon, but it would make a great hat." "Captured running wild on the prairie near Kearney, Nebraska – we have a standing offer of $10,000 to anyone who can identify the specie". "Not stuffed – not petrified – alive and living on the inside". Perhaps as a defense against possible skepticism – this is a carnival, after all – just being "alive" or just being "living" was not sufficient assurance. The double, though redundant, reinforcement of "alive and living" seemed necessary.

In the first 50 years of the nineteen-hundreds it was not unusual for carnivals to feature as many shows as rides. The great Art B. Thomas Shows out of Lennox, South Dakota advertised for the 1937 season – "The Bombshell of 1937 – Ten Rides – Ten Shows". It was not unusual for a big carnival to carry a full variety show with a live band of eight to ten pieces.

When these variety shows had an all colored cast – as they often did – they were called "Jig Shows". The well- known stripper, Sally Rand, travelled with the Royal American Shows for a time. As recently as the early sixties, Merriam's Midway Shows played the Poinsett County Fair in Harrisburg, Arkansas with four separate girl shows on the midway. The number of rides was probably ten, but that included two Ferris wheels. With the two wheels side by side, centered in the backend of the midway, and flanked by two girl shows on either side this was "big carnival".

Merriam's almost missed the era of big side shows. The venues played just did not have the population and revenue potential to support the high overhead and payroll that the large cast variety shows faced. But, the spirit of American showmanship was alive and well (even alive and living) and Merriam's had its shows.

Pete Leslie: (early fifties)

As best memory serves Pete Leslie was from Des Moines, Iowa, and was around the show for three or four years in the period just after the partnership with Robinson was dissolved. Pete Leslie had the first of the few snake shows on Merriam's. The star attraction, the snake, was a boa constrictor that would lie sleeping in a cage in the center of the tent while live mice walked around inside the cage, waiting to be dinner for the snake. It was a big snake – probably about eight to ten feet long – and for Iowans in 1950 it was probably worth the twenty-five cents admission to see. The free show outside should also be considered part of the attraction.

Pete sold tickets from an open topped ticket booth always dressed in matching khakis, polished brown boots and a pith helmet. The shirt had huge button down pockets and shoulder epaulettes. His neckwear for the outfit was a live bull snake about four feet in length and was actually quite active. It would crawl around on Pete's neck and shoulders watching him sell tickets and giving the customers the thrill of being up close and personal with a live snake. The show tent, itself, was probably about ten feet by twenty with a thirty foot three section banner line. There were three pictorial banners – the center one shorter to allow space for the ticket booth and an entrance and exit area - showing giant snakes crushing wide eyed, black African natives and doing battle with lions, tigers and other jungle creatures. Around Pete's neck, along with the snake, was a microphone, black taped to a clothes hanger so he could bally the show and sell tickets at the same time.

Pete had a wife, whose first name has been lost to oral history, and daughter, Carlene, who was about Dale's age. That would put the two of them about ten or eleven at the time. One season, at the Kossuth County Fair in Algona, Iowa there seemed to be a native population of wild garter snakes on the fairgrounds. During set up, Dale and Carlene, discovered a nest of baby snakes. In that nest of, maybe, twenty baby snakes they found a live (yes, alive and living) baby snake with two heads. Well, this, the kids thought was going to be the second greatest attraction alongside of the giant boa constrictor. With a fruit jar and a handful of grass their zoological oddity was proudly presented to Carlene's father, and the two-headed snake was exhibited in the show. Unfortunately the poor creature only lived a few days, but for a while it was a living two-headed snake.

Pete's other show was a "Whatizit" animal show. This show was similar in size and design to the snake show. The pictorial banners showed a weasel looking critter with huge fangs and claws with big question marks overlaid on the pictorial. The banner over the ticket booth made the offer of a reward to anyone who could identify the animal. The animal was a kudamundi from Central America. Related to the ring-tailed lemur, the most remarkable thing about the kudamundi is that they were little known in the United States. They were for sale in the classified section of Billboard magazine making it fairly easy for anyone to get into the "Whatizit" business. If it added to the enjoyment experienced by the local fairgoers to be told the critter was "captured on the open prairie near Kearney, Nebraska, what's the harm. There is no known record of anyone collecting the reward for correctly identifying the animal.

John – The Stone Man (early fifties)

John was truly a unique attraction and was around Merriam's for a couple of years. The banners and the bally advertised a man slowly turning to stone. "A scientific marvel – a medical mystery" "A living, breathing human being slowly turning to stone before you very eyes." "Touch him." "Talk to him." "Be amazed at what you touch and hear." Whatever his medical condition was, it was real. If not stone, his feet and legs felt as hard as stone. John was paralyzed from the waist down with some movement of his arms and head. He did his own bally dressed only in shorts with the microphone laying on his chest. He would invite viewers to hold on to his big toe as he talked. His toe would vibrate as the sound of his voice vibrated though the solid lower part of his body. At the end of the evenings work his wife and hired man would carry John back to his house trailer. No cot or stretcher was needed. John was stiff as a board. His wife would take his feet and the hired man would take the shoulders and carry him to the trailer like a log.

During this time period, Dale was the Billboard agent on the show. Billboard was the weekly news magazine for the entertainment industry – carnivals, circuses, grandstand acts and the recording industry. Dale would order the required number of Billboards each week and have them for sale or deliver them to his customers. John was one of those customers. When the Billboards came in Dale would deliver one to John. There he would be lying on his back just as he had been placed the night before. John had a terrible medical disability but he seemed to have a loving wife and he was in show business.

Gene and Catherine Woods (thirties – forties – fifties)

One of the big changes in the carnival business in the last fifty years has been the narrowing of age group of its customer base. The loss of the appeal of the shows has a lot to do with that narrowing. It once was that there was something to appeal to every age group. If a three generational family came to the fair the midway had some form of entertainment for each family member. The rides, of course, for the children and grand-children. Merry-go-rounds and kiddie cars for the smaller ones, tilt-a-whirls for those a little older, and a romantic Ferris wheel ride for teenage couples each filled their niche. Fathers and grandfathers could enjoy a little gambling at one of the percentage games like the pan game or the checker board dart. The more athletic men had ball games or the high-striker. The women – mother and grandmother – could sit and play bingo by the hour while the rest of the family did their things.

One of those "things" – for the grown men – might just be to take in one of the girl shows on the midway. Little Egypt started it all at the great Columbian Exposition in Chicago, and girl shows were a part of the midway experience for at least the first seventy-five years. The book Girl Show by A.W. Stencell is a well written and well researched history of carnival girl shows, and makes good reading about this slice of show business. From its beginning in the mid-thirties until the mid to late fifties the girl show spot was filled by Gene Woods and his wife Catherine. They were there before Dale was born, and later Catherine was Dale's sometime baby sitter. In the early years Catherine was the "girl" in the show and Gene the talker and ticket seller. By the time Dale was about ten and Margret was born they had a hired "girl" so Catherine didn't have to "work".

Gene and Catherine were from Rathbun, Iowa – six miles north of Centerville – in the southeast part of the state. Gene's slow and easy going mannerisms would seem to place him, perhaps, from somewhere like southeast Georgia. During the off hours Gene would gather the show children around him and tell them long and rambling stories about Peter Rabbit. He made up the stories as he went along with intricate plots that had twists and turns and always happy endings. His deep, slow drawl made his voice equally good for story telling as well as "talking" on the show bally and describing the attributes of the lovely Patsy and the dance she would perform on the inside. The girl's name was always Patsy because that was what was painted on the banners on the show front. Just how naughty and revealing that show was, Dale was never quite sure. Grandma Myrtle claimed, "they took off all their clothes", and Dale shouldn't think about it.

As the sun began to set and the midway lights came on if mom and grandma had a little more egg money left to play a few more cards of bingo, the "grown men" might wander down to the back end of the midway where they would hear Gene begin his bally. "It's showtime, it's showtime, it's showtime for the men and the men only. As I said this show is for the men and the men only between the ages of eighteen and eighty. If you're under the age of eighteen you wouldn't understand it and if you are over eighty – well – you simply couldn't stand it. Yes, it's almost showtime where they shake it to the east and shake it to the west, but it's inside where they shake it the best. Yes, gentlemen, line right up and get your tickets now because they're going to twitch it and twotch it and let you big boys watch it. You say you don't know if the show is worth the price of admission.

You say you don't k now if it is worth one half of one dollar. Let me tell you about the dance lovely Patsy will perform for you on the inside and you make up your own mind." Pointing to Patsy's neck and head, Gene would continue. "I'll admit from the neck on up nothing much is going to happen." Then indicating her knees, he would go on. "And, likewise, from the knees on down not much is going to happen." Then, with added excitement and indicating her breasts and hips, he would continue. "But, believe me brothers, somewhere between the Appalachian mountains and Happy Valley all hell is going to break loose! Buy your tickets now – It's showtime!"

On the drive home the whole family had been entertained. Tummies ached from cotton candy, hot dogs and tilt-a-whirl rides, the stop on top of the Ferris wheel was alone worth the price of admission, the women had won a Beacon blanket playing bingo, the men had won or lost a few dollars at the pan game, and then there was Patsy.

Chief Little Wolf (the fifties)

Still another show that had wide appeal and one that the adult men enjoyed was the "At show". "At" was an abbreviation or slang for athletic. The athletic show featured wrestling and boxing matches ostensibly between the champion (in this case, Chief Little Wolf) on the bally platform and the local challenger who comes up from the crowd. Wrestling is usually the chosen sport probably because it is easier to prolong the drama and no one is as likely to get a black eye or a bloody nose.

The show tent resembles the ones previously described except for size. Chief's At show top was probably thirty by fifty with a sixty foot banner line. The pictorials showed grossly over muscular men engaged in wrestling, boxing and other contact sports. The banner over the ticket booth read, "Athletic Arena Nobody Barred". Again, as the sun set and the evening crowd started to build Chief Little Wolf would step up on the bally platform and begin to beat a steady but driving tempo on his war drum. It was then that the official challenge would be made. Chief Little Wolf would claim, "I've never been beaten in the state of Minnesota. That makes me the champion of Minnesota". The challenger in the crowd below would challenge back with, "You've never beaten me!". With that, the challenger would leap on the bally platform, raise his arms in the air and offer his own challenge against Chief. At that time mom might continue to place kernels of corn on her bingo card and give dad nodding approval to see what all the commotion was in the backend.

APPENDIX

AND THEN THERE WAS ....
MEMORIES AND THOUGHTS

Authors thoughts:

There are those (including myself) who thought I spent way too much time in the writing of this book. On the other hand, in my defense, I was remembering, savoring those memories, and reliving my and other peoples' lives. People who lived lives closely connected with and intertwined with my own. Surely, critics wouldn't argue that too much time was spent living these lives, so why not spend the time required to discuss and describe the lives as they were lived.

These thoughts, stories, people and events and mini bios came to mind somewhat randomly, not fitting any particular time or category. They are necessary, however, to flavor and complete the total story. These are not listed in any order of importance or significance. I know, when I finally type the elusive words, THE END a thought will appear in my head that begins, "And then there was...".

And then there was... Andy Saban.

Andy Saban graduated from McClintock High School in Tempe, Arizona, and was a good friend of Todd's. Both graduated in the class of 1984. Andy was neat, clean and precise, almost to a fault. He liked the girls (and they liked him), but he couldn't quite envision one cluttering up his life in any permanent way. Also, it would not be right to place him in any one of these previously casted roles – rideboy, jointee, etc. He's done them all to a large and small extent. Again, also, it would not be right to cast him in the side kick role. Both Dale and Todd had and needed sidekicks – perhaps Dale more than Todd – but need them they did.

Andy's first job was driving a pineapple truck in Hawaii. He also was a parking valet at some swanky, up-state New York Inn. Always, however, staying in touch with Todd and feeling the gentle tug of show business on his heart and eager young muscles. The "Glory Years" of the 1980s were well suited to a young man who lived just enough of a fantasy to welcome being sent on knightly duties out to conquer emperors. These would include working the sales window in the corn dog or being promoted to Tilt foreman in the middle of a teardown.

Andy's role on the carnival was to basically do anything he was asked. He had a great attitude and thoroughly enjoyed his experience. In the summer 1985, Andy worked in Hawaii, driving pineapple trucks for half the day and surfing for the other half of the day. He was in paradise and loved everything about his situation. Through a series of phone calls, Todd Merriam convinced him to leave his luxurious life in Hawaii to become a rideboy on Merriam's Midway Shows. That very next summer, Andy came out on the carnival and was there every summer for the next 20 plus years.

And then there was…. Bruce Carlson

Bruce Carlson from Ogden Iowa was surely a game changer as far as the growth of the show goes. Bruce's parent's house was just across the street east from Web and Myrtle Merriam's property and the show winter quarters, perfect to catch the eye and heart of a teenage boy. He started working part time at the show winter quarters on weekends after the show opened in Perry. Al wouldn't let him work if it took him out of school. What a valuable school he was already attending, learning from and watching Al and Web drill, paint and weld. With this background Bruce was ready to continue on to the operation of rides like the Scrambler, Trabant and others. Bruce, as it turned out, had a natural talent for this type of work. He stayed with the show when Dale took over and helped to take the show into the electric age. Bruce started out as a rideboy and transitioned into being the show's electrician. The carnival nickname for the electrician has always been "Sparky". That nickname soon attached itself to Bruce. His ability to literally fix anything made him an invaluable member of the staff for decades. Bruce was on the show for 40 plus years and was an integral part of it's growth.

Bruce married Kathy Bednar from Austin MN. They had two children. "Kathy B" ran the machine gun joint allowing Bruce to continue being the show electrician. They are currently with Evan's United Shows.

And then there was….. Roy Armstrong

The Sky wheel was advertised as "The King of the Midway" by Chance Manufacturing Company. When Roy took over as foreman of the sky wheel he took over control of the King and was awarded the title of "Sir Roy" at one of the season ending awards parties. Roy was probably as close to a true "professional" rideboy as there could be. First of all, he had the credentials. He had a CDL and years of hands-on training with various carnivals. He simply had the experience and the skills to do his job. In addition, he had the calm temperament when times got stressful. His wife Connie was the queen of the Popper.

And then there was….. Ferris wheel George

Ferris wheel George was a classic. He could stand at the clutch of the Eli Wheel hour after hour without a relief man. Many times he would actually turn away his relief man. He took great pride in his knowledge and skill as foreman of the Wheel. George ran the wheel through the mid 80's. By this time the ropes to be pulled were limited to putting in 9 spokes on the Wheel. When he pulled those ropes it was with the pride of a wheel man. He always had the same appearance. He wore a red show hat, overalls, black steel toed boots. In his mouth he always had a huge dip of Copenhagen chewing tobacco and very few teeth. He had a grumpy sort of countenance to him, but from time to time, you could see him smile at the kids as they were excitedly loading onto the ride.

And then there was….. Mickie Launderville

Mickie Launderville was probably the last of the next generation Tilt men. He viewed setting up and tearing down as a sporting event to be timed, cheered for, compared and bragged about. Mickie was probably the last Tilt man that rode the intermediate platforms while the tilt was running. (Not a good practice, but almost irresistible for Mickie). Mickie was the "Rock Star" type of rideboy. He worked hard and partied harder. Every night, Mickie was up until the sun came up getting drunk, falling asleep at dawn, and waking up just in time to hear the song, "back in the saddle again" playing on the Merry go Round opening the show, usually around 12 noon or 1pm. Mickie, who usually slept in the cab of a truck every night, amongst his dirty clothes, would hear the song, jump up, put fresh water on his head and get out to the ride to take tickets and buck tubs.

And then there was….. Mark Samuels

Mark Samuels was a true gift to the show from the Sherril family of West Bend, Iowa. The Sherril's, (Stan & Donna), had a sizable game operation with the show during the 70's and 80's. Mark followed Ferris wheel George as the wheel foreman. He was one of those types of rideboys that would tear down and setup numerous rides until the show was completely setup or torn down. As the years went by, he became the foreman of the zipper. He always had a positive attitude and his multi-ride experience made him an invaluable member of the staff for decades. Mark was on the show for over 35 years and his loyalty to Dale was without question. Mark currently drives trucks for a living and continues to be in contact with the Merriam family up until this day.

And then there was ….. Bill Samuels

Bill Samuels, "Billy", Mark's younger brother, was another valued gift from the Sherrill family. Like his brother Mark, he was another one of those invaluable rideboys that would setup and tear down any ride that needed it, as well as tackling any tasks that Dale asked of him. He was the foreman of the Scrambler and once he tore down that ride, he'd converge on the Merry-go-round, the Wheel, the Tilt, and as the sun was coming up, the floor of the Bumper Cars. He also worked closely with Bruce Carlson, helping with all of the wire and electrical equipment. In Bruce's two year absence from the show, Billy took over as Electrician of the show. He now works and lives in Janesville MN as an insurance salesman.

And then there was…...Bing and Kathy Bucher

Bing and Kathy Bucher were from Zumbrota Minnesota. Bing knew Alicia from the High School days around the Pine Island, Minnesota area. Somehow, Bing and Kathy got into the Carnival food service, and booked their mini-donuts with the Merriam's. One of the first dates they played was the Mitchel Corn Palace. Kathy was a trained Accountant, and kept books for Dale a couple of years during the 90's. Janesville Minnesota was also a good spot for the mini-donuts. The mini-donut lovers were faithful customers. One year when Bing and Kathy couldn't make the date, disappointed Janesville customers would holler in the corn dog window, "where are the god damn mini-donuts". This brings to mind another well remembered Jointees phrase.

The spot was Anoka, and the event was a sudden afternoon windstorm. Concessionaire, Roger Kahoot and his crew, were desperately trying to save their concessions and prizes. Teddy Bears and other prizes were being desperately loaded into trucks, and other places of safety. Roger, all five foot six of him, with straw hat and sandals, leading the salvage operation he saw the futility of his efforts. He could be heard from one end of the Midway to the other, "Fuck the stock, run for your lives".

And then there was …. Roger Kavern

Roger Kavern was the typical side kick type person for Dale. He would do anything that Dale asked of him and showed authority when he did it. Hop along Cassidy had "California Carlson", Roy Rodgers had Gabby Hayes, The lone Ranger had Tonto and Dale Merriam had Roger Kavern. Roger was aka "Mr. Coffee". He could stop what he was doing and go for coffee quicker than any man alive. He loved the business and served Dale well during the middle years. His sideline was a novelty joint. When asked what he did for Dale, it was a hard question to answer, but he did it well. He would fuel trucks, take trucks to repair shops, assist in laying out the lot, recruit and assign help and report any important information to Dale about what he would hear and see when observing the staff. He was on the show during the missing decade and came back during the mid 80's through the mid 90's.

And then there was…. Glen Zobbell

Glen Zobbell was from Fredericksburg Iowa. Fredericksburg was a two day spot. One of those spots you weren't in long enough to unhook a trailer. When Glen was a teenager, he would hire on a work as extra help, probably at a $1.25 per hour. He almost always worked on the wheel. He was a farmer but always found time to come help setup and teardown the midway. At about age 60 he quit farming and asked Dale if he could come on the road with the show and be the shop foreman. Dale still has the rusty folded up metal chair with the name "Glen" squalled on the back. There's nothing that you couldn't ask Glen to do. He had a great attitude, loved to work and was a good friend.

And then there was…. The Sherrill's

Stan and Donna Sherrill from West Bend Iowa brought their entire family out on the carnival every summer for decades. They produced multiple game concessions every year. Both Stan and Donna were school teachers. Tina was a star girl's basketball player, Theresa worked with Alicia in the Carnival office, Trudy and Tim were both game agents. Trudy married Bobby West and they began operating their own line up of games. The Sherrill's were also responsible for introducing three members of the Samuel's family that were all important to the carnival, those being Mary Ellen, who was a faithful ticket box seller along with her two sons, Mark and Billy. The Sherrill's began during the end of the missing decade and were with the carnival for 30 plus years.

And then there was…. Mitchell and Martha Buxton

Mitchell and Martha Buxton were from Austin Minnesota. They are the longest tenured jointees on the show without a doubt. They also produced the most joints out of all other jointees for Merriam's Midway Shows throughout the decades. They slipped through the edges of the missing decade and were there waiting for their location in 1974 when Dale took over. Mitchell was a past president of the Midwest Showmen's Association. They were great friends and business partners and it was through their involvement with the show, that Matt Anderson, Dale's son in law, met and married his daughter Trissa. Matt and Trissa are owners of joints and games on Merriam's Midway Shows to this day.

Merriam's Front Gate, circa 1950 Midway features
new 1948 Allan Herschell merry-go-round.

With the edition of the Hurricane, thrill rides are beginning to take over.

The Zipper became one of the most popular rides on the show.

Dale's office patriotically painted for the 1976 route.

The undisputed King of the Midway allowing our
staff to display the new show colors.

Canon Ball Smith, of Halfway, Missouri, prepares to slide down the barrel of
his canon to be shot over the top of both Ferris wheels. Always a crowd pleaser,
Canon Ball played several County & State fairs around the turn of the century.

Three generations – Al congratulates his son Dale on becoming
the new show owner, and Grandson, Todd on becoming
the Heir Apparent. There's no business like it!

Show owner, Dale Merriam proudly points out features of
the new Hy-V Eli wheel to father, Al Merriam.

New logos.

New Mexico State Fair 2000.

Dale & Alicia Merriam Grand Marshall's in the Pine
Island Minnesota Cheese Festival parade

Still No Fence

HOLIDAY JOY

THE MERRIAMS
Dale, Alicia, Tommy, Trissa, Todd

EPILOGUE

What you have just read is the story of an American Carnival that spanned over 7 decades. The 1900's were the "American Century" and the traveling carnival was certainly an American industry. From the first Ferris Wheel, at the Chicago World's fair in 1893, carrying on into the 20th century by the likes of Buffalo Bill, Sally Rand and Midway presentations at county and state fairs nation-wide, the American Carnival flourished from humble beginnings.

Merriam's Midway Shows was born in the mid 30's when Wilbur Merriam and his son Alva first dreamed of a livelihood that could be gained outside of their farm in Titonka Iowa. They were not alone in this endeavor. All over the United States, the American Carnival was taking root, and the first national trade association for the Carnival industry, the OABA, had as their slogan, "Dedicated to the Preservation of America's Agricultural Fairs".

Merriam's Rides, the name of Wilbur and Alva's first attempt into the carnival business, consisted of 3, hand crafted, drive-'em-yourself cars. From hand carved wooden horses to midways full of SkyWheels and Thunderbolts, Wilbur may not have imagined the potential that was packaged up in those first 3 small cars. This small spark that he started would later become his son's, grandson's and great grandson's families' livelihoods for the next 70 years, bringing joy and happiness into the lives of multiple thousands of people.

The appeal of the American Carnival is well into it's 2nd Century and continues to be passed from generation to generation. This is just as true for the owners and operators as it is for the fun seeking crowd. Nothing can quite compare to the thrill of the changing of the direction of your body, accelerating and spinning in the seat of the Tilt-a-whirl, or the feeling you have at the top of the Giant Ferris Wheel as you look across the entirety of the Midway below, or better than both of those experiences, riding with your girlfriend and giving her a little squeeze.

May the fun last forever…..

So bring on the wooden horses and the iron men.

Merriam & Robinson Shows
Permanent Address: Ogden, Iowa, Phone 456
1948 ROUTE

CARNIVAL — Boone, Iowa	May 3-8
FOREST PARK CARNIVAL — Marshalltown, Iowa	May 10-15
AMERICAN LEGION CARNIVAL — Jefferson, Iowa	May 17-22
FIREMANS CARNIVAL — Allio, Iowa	May 24-29
JR. CHAMBER OF COMMERCE CARNIVAL — Fairfield, Iowa	May 31-June 5
AMERICAN LEGION CELEBRATION — Manillo, Iowa	June 7-8-9
V.F.W. CELEBRATION — Ida Grove, Iowa	June 11-12
OPEN	June 14-17
FIREMANS CELEBRATION — Radcliffe, Iowa	June 18-19
CARNIVAL — Perry, Iowa	June 21-22-23
V.F.W.-AMER. LEGION CELEBRATION — Panora, Iowa	June 24-25-26
AMERICAN LEGION CELEBRATION — Odeboit, Iowa	June 28-29-30
AMERICAN LEGION CELEBRATION — Gowrie, Iowa	July 1-2-3
CHAMBER OF COMMERCE CELEBRATION — Boone, Iowa	July 4-5
AMERICAN LEGION CELEBRATION — Woodward, Iowa	July 6-9-10
OPEN	July 13-16
OPEN	July 18-22
V.F.W. CELEBRATION — Sheffield, Iowa	July 27-28
AMERICAN LEGION CELEBRATION — Greene, Iowa	July 30-31
GRUNDY COUNTY FAIR — Grundy Center, Iowa	August 4-7
FIREMANS CELEBRATION — State Center, Iowa	August 9-10-11
CENTENNIAL CELEBRATION — Montezuma, Iowa	August 12-13-14
HOBO DAYS — Britt, Iowa	August 16-17
DIAMOND JUBILEE — Traer, Iowa	August 18-21
FRANKLIN COUNTY FAIR — Hampton, Iowa	August 22-24
MADISON COUNTY FAIR — Madison, Nebraska	August 25-30
PLATTE COUNTY FAIR — Columbus, Nebraska	Aug. 31-Sept. 1-5
HOWARD COUNTY FAIR — St. Paul, Nebraska	Sept. 8-11
STANTON COUNTY FAIR — Stanton, Nebraska	Sept. 12-14
WAYNE COUNTY FAIR — Wayne, Nebraska	Sept. 15-18
JOHNSON COUNTY FAIR — Tecumseh, Nebraska	Sept. 20-25
CORN SHOW AND FESTIVAL — Adel, Iowa	Sept. 29-Oct. 1-2

The 1948 Route Card for Merriam & Robinson Shows is the only one known to be in existence. The hand notations were made by Al Merriam in preparation of the printing of the 1949 Cards. It is interesting to note how many of the dates remained with Merriam, and are on the 1949 route. Britt, Iowa Hobo Days – a good spot – went with Robinson. Merriam, however, retained the majority.

Merriam's Midway Shows
Permanent Address: Ogden, Iowa, Phone 456
1949 ROUTE

CARNIVAL — Boone, Iowa	May 3-7
FOREST PARK CARNIVAL — Marshalltown, Iowa	May 9-15
AMVETS CARNIVAL — Iowa Falls, Iowa	May 17-21
LEGION DAYS CELEBRATION (Street) — Jefferson, Iowa	May 17-21
AMERICAN LEGION SPRING FROLIC — Colfax, Iowa	May 24-25
V.F.W. CARNIVAL — Nevada, Iowa	May 27-28
AMERICAN LEGION CELEBRATION — Manilla, Iowa	May 30-June 4
V.F.W. CELEBRATION — Panora, Iowa	June 6-8
V.F.W. CELEBRATION — Kamrada, Iowa	June 9-11
FIREMAN'S CELEBRATION — Radcliffe, Iowa	June 14-15
EGG DAY CELEBRATION — Alden, Iowa	June 17-18
COMMUNITY CLUB "BIG DAYS" — Sheffield, Iowa	June 21-22
AMERICAN LEGION CELEBRATION — Odeboit, Iowa	June 23-25
4TH OF JULY CELEBRATION — Gowrie, Iowa	June 27-29
AMERICAN LEGION CELEBRATION — Woodward, Iowa	July 4
AMERICAN LEGION CELEBRATION — Jewell, Iowa	July 7-9
OPEN	July 11-13
AMERICAN LEGION CELEBRATION — Greene, Iowa	July 14-16
OPEN	July 19-20
STATE CENTER FALL FESTIVAL — State Center, Iowa	July 21-23
LEGION FUN DAYS — Ogden, Iowa	July 25-27
GRUNDY CO. FAIR — Grundy Center, Iowa	July 28-30
SAUERKRAUT DAYS — Arkley, Iowa	August 3-6
RICE COUNTY FAIR — Faribault, Minnesota	August 8-9
KOSSUTH CO. FAIR — Algona, Iowa	August 11-14
BURT COUNTY FAIR — Oakland, Nebraska	August 17-20
PLATTE CO. FAIR — Columbus, Nebraska	August 24-27
53RD ANNUAL LABOR DAY CELEBRATION — Graettinger, Iowa	Aug. 30-Sept. 2
OSCEOLA CO. FAIR — Sibley, Iowa	Sept. 5
STANTON CO. FAIR — Stanton, Nebraska	Sept. 6-9
WAYNE CO. FAIR — Wayne, Nebraska	Sept. 11-13
JOHNSON CO. FAIR — Tecumseh, Nebraska	Sept. 14-17
FALL FAIR AND STREET FESTIVAL — Iowa Falls, Iowa	Sept. 19-22
CORN SHOW AND FESTIVAL — Adel, Iowa	Sept. 27-28
	Sept. 29-Oct. 1

By the Spring of 1949, Harry S. Truman had taken office in his own elected right, and Al had a full five month route booked for the inaugural season of Merriam's Midway Shows.

... RIDES ...

- BIG ELI FERRIS WHEEL
- MERRY-GO-ROUND
- OCT-O-PUS
- TILT-A-WHIRL
- KIDDIE AUTO RIDE
- LITTLE TRAIN

... SHOWS ...

- MONKEY LAND
- LITTLE FARM
- GOOD NIGHT IRENE
- FUN HOUSE

ATTRACTIONS

- LIGHT TOWERS
- MAIN ENTRANCE

CONCESSIONS

25 NEW AND IMPROVED
AMUSEMENT GAMES

OUR 1950 ROUTE

BOONE, IOWA	May 1-13
ATLANTIC, IOWA, Anvets Carnival	May 15-30
ALBIA, IOWA, Fireman's Carnival	May 22-27
JEFFERSON, IOWA, Legion Days	May 29-31
COLFAX, IOWA, Legion Celebration	June 2-3
KANAWHA, IOWA, Legion Celebration	June 6-7
RADCLIFFE, IOWA, Firemen's Celebration	June 9-10
MANILLA, IOWA, Legion Celebration	June 12-14
PANORA, IOWA, VFW Celebration	June 15-17
FREDERICKSBURG, IOWA, Dairy Days	June 19-20
NEW HAMPTON, IOWA	June 21-24
READLYN, IOWA, Commercial Club Celebration	June 26-28
CANNON FALLS, MINN., Cannon Valley Fair	July 3-4
LAKE CITY, MINN., Legion Carnival	July 6-8
PLAINVIEW, MINN., Legion Carnival	July 10-11-12
WINONA, MINN., Steamboat Days	July 13-15
REDWING, MINN., Fireman's Festival	July 16-22
GRAND MEADOW, MINN., Harvest Festival	July 24-29
FOUNTAIN, MINN., Harvest Festival	July 27-29
ACKLEY, IOWA, Sauerkraut Days	Aug. 1-3
OGDEN, IOWA, Free Fun Days	Aug. 4-5
GRUNDY CENTER, IOWA, Grundy County Fair	Aug. 7-9
TRAER, IOWA, 4-H Fair & Celebration	Aug. 10-12
TITONKA, IOWA, Indian Days	Aug. 14-13
ALGONA, IOWA, Kossuth County Fair	Aug. 16-19
HAMPTON, IOWA, Franklin Co. Fair	Aug. 20-23
OAKLAND, NEBR., Burt County Fair	Aug. 24-26
COLUMBUS, NEBR., Platte County Fair	Aug. 29-Sept. 1
SCHUYLER, NEBR., Labor Day Celebration	Sept. 2-4
GUTHRIE CENTER, IOWA, Guthrie County Fair	Sept. 5-8
STANTON, NEBR., Stanton Co. Fair	Sept. 10-15
WAYNE, NEBR., Wayne Co. Fair	Sept. 13-16
IOWA FALLS, IOWA, Street Fair and Festival	Sept. 18-20
PERRY, IOWA, Diamond Jubilee Festival	Sept. 21-23
DENVER, IOWA, Sauerkraut Days	Sept. 26-27
PRESTON, MINN., Celebration	Sept. 29-30

Merriam's Midway Shows
1950 ROUTE CARD

BOONE, IOWA	MAY 15-17
TAMA, IOWA	MAY 19-24
CARROLL, IOWA	MAY 26-31
ATLANTIC, IOWA	JUNE 2-3-4
WEBSTER CITY, IOWA	JUNE 5-6
ODEBOLT, IOWA	JUNE 9-10-11
POMEROY, IOWA	JUNE 13-14
FREDERICKSBURG, IOWA	JUNE 16-17
GRAND MEADOW, MINN.	JUNE 18-20-21
OPEN	JUNE 23-24-25
PAYNESVILLE, MINN.	JUNE 26-27-28
MOUNTAIN LAKE, MINN.	JUNE 30-JULY 1
CANNON FALLS, MINN.	JULY 2-3-4
ISLE, MINN.	JULY 6-7-8
CAMBRIDGE, MINN.	JULY 10-11-12
PARK RAPIDS, MINN.	JULY 14-15-16
PINE ISLAND, MINN.	JULY 18-19-20
CANBY, MINN.	JULY 21-22-23
SLEEPY EYE, MINN.	JULY 25-26-27
TITONKA, IOWA	JULY 28-30
OGDEN, IOWA	AUG. 1-2
VINTON, IOWA	AUG. 4-7
WAUKON, IOWA	AUG. 8-9-10
ALGONA, IOWA	AUG. 12-15
WELLS, MINN.	AUG. 16-17
WEST UNION, IOWA	AUG. 19-22
COLUMBUS, NEB.	AUG. 23-29
SCHUYLER, NEB.	AUG. 30-31-SEPT. 1
GUTHRIE CENTER, IOWA	SEPT. 2-6
SCRIBNER, NEB.	SEPT. 9-12
BRAINARD, NEB.	SEPT. 13-14
MILFORD, NEB.	SEPT. 15-16
COZAD, NEB.	SEPT. 18-19
GOTHENBURG, NEB.	SEPT. 22-24-25

You will like us alright as we are
just having a town here in the
An... at ...

Al, Edna, Da... argret,
Dad and ...ther

MERRIAM'S
MIDWAY SHOWS
OF
OGDEN, IOWA

PRESENT FOR 1951

4 - SHOWS - 4

---

8 - RIDES - 8

---

25 - CONCESSIONS - 25

"YOU'VE TRIED THE REST,
NOW TRY THE BEST"

Merriam's Midway Shows
1952 ROUTE CARD

ALBIA, IOWA	MAY 9-12
TAMA, IOWA	MAY 14-15
PERRY, IOWA	MAY 21-28
COLUMBUS, NEB.	MAY 29-JUNE 2
VINTON, IOWA	JUNE 5-8
FREDERICKSBURG, IOWA	JUNE 11-12
WACONIA, MINN.	JUNE 14-16-17
LAKEFIELD, MINN.	JUNE 18-20
WILLMAR, MINN.	JUNE 21-22-23
MOUNTAIN LAKE, MINN.	JUNE 25-26
FOUNTAIN, MINN.	JUNE 28-29-30
CANNON FALLS, MINN.	JULY 2-3-4
BLOOMING PRAIRIE, MINN.	JULY 6-7-8
DETROIT LAKES, MINN.	JULY 12-15
PARK RAPIDS, MINN.	JULY 16-17-18
PINE ISLAND, MINN.	JULY 20-21-22
GRAND MEADOW, MINN.	JULY 23-24-25
SLEEPY EYE, MINN.	JULY 27-28-29
OGDEN, IOWA	JULY 31-AUG. 1
MISSOURI VALLEY, IOWA	AUG. 2-3-4
ALTA, IOWA	AUG. 8-9
BELMOND, IOWA	AUG. 15-11
TITONKA, IOWA	AUG. 13
ALGONA, IOWA	AUG. 14-17
SAC CITY, IOWA	AUG. 19-22
STANTON, NEB.	AUG. 24-25
COLUMBUS, NEB.	AUG. 29-31
SCHUYLER, NEB.	SEPT. 1-2-3
MOVILLE, IOWA	SEPT. 5-6
COZAD, NEB.	SEPT. 13-14
CURTIS, NEB.	SEPT. 15-16
GOTHENBURG, NEB.	SEPT. 19-20
GREENFIELD, IOWA	SEPT. 22-24

136

Merriam's Midway Shows
Ogden, Iowa

1853 Route

ATLANTIC, IOWA	May 4-9
WEBSTER CITY, IOWA	May 11-16
MARSHALLTOWN, IOWA	May 18-24
DENISON, IOWA	May 27-30
ALBIA, IOWA	June 1-3
COLFAX, IOWA	June 4-6
OTTUMWA, IOWA	June 8-13
FREDERICKSBURG, IOWA	June 15-16
DENVER, IOWA	June 18-20
SHERBURN, MINNESOTA	June 22-24
WILLMAR, MINNESOTA	June 25-27
MOUNTAIN LAKE, MINNESOTA	June 29-30
CANNON FALLS, MINNESOTA	July 2-4
GRAND MEADOW, MINNESOTA	July 6-8
BLOOMING PRAIRIE, MINNESOTA	July 10-12
NORTHFIELD, MINNESOTA	July 14-18
CLARA CITY, MINNESOTA	July 20-22
BUFFALO, MINNESOTA	July 23-25
MANSON, IOWA	July 27-29
OGDEN, IOWA	July 31-Aug. 1
INDIANOLA, IOWA	Aug. 3-5
GRUNDY CENTER, IOWA	Aug. 6-8
IDA GROVE, IOWA	Aug. 10-12
DENISON, IOWA	Aug. 13-16
ALGONA, IOWA	Aug. 19-22
SAC CITY, IOWA	Aug. 24-26
BLOOMFIELD, NEBRASKA	Aug. 28-30
COLUMBUS, NEBRASKA	Sept. 1-4
SCHUYLER, NEBRASKA	Sept. 5-7
GUTHRIE CENTER, IOWA	Sept. 9-11
STANTON, NEBRASKA	Sept. 13-15
ALBION, NEBRASKA	Sept. 16-19
COZAD, NEBRASKA	Sept. 23-24
	Sept. 28-Oct. 3

Merriam's Midway Shows

1857 ROUTE

ALBIA, IOWA	MAY 1-4
TAMA, IOWA	MAY 6-11
BOONE, IOWA	MAY 13-18
	MAY 20-25
ATLANTIC, IOWA	MAY 27-JUNE 1
VINTON, IOWA	JUNE 3-5
BELMOND, IOWA	JUNE 7-8
ODEBOLT, IOWA	JUNE 10-12
OGDEN, IOWA	JUNE 14-15
FREDERICKSBURG, IOWA	JUNE 17-18
WACONIA, MINN.	JUNE 21-23
MOUNTAIN LAKE, MINN.	JUNE 24-25
PAYNESVILLE, MINN.	JUNE 27-29
CANNON FALLS, MINN.	JULY 2-3-4
BLOOMING PRAIRIE, MINN.	JULY 5-6-7
	JULY 9-11
PINE ISLAND, MINN.	JULY 12-14
CANBY, MINN.	JULY 17-20
PARK RAPIDS, MINN.	JULY 22-24
SLEEPY EYE, MINN.	JULY 26-28
TITONKA, IOWA	JULY 29-30
MISSOURI VALLEY, IOWA	AUG. 1-2
ALTA, IOWA	AUG. 5-8
ROCK RAPIDS, IOWA	AUG. 9-11
ALGONA, IOWA	AUG. 13-16
SAC CITY, IOWA	AUG. 18-21
OAKLAND, NEB.	AUG. 22-24
COLUMBUS, NEB.	AUG. 26-29
SCHUYLER, NEB.	AUG. 31-SEPT. 2
GUTHRIE CENTER, IOWA	SEPT. 2-5
SCRIBNER, NEB.	SEPT. 10-13
MILFORD, NEB.	SEPT. 16-17
COZAD, NEB.	SEPT. 18-20

Merriam Midway Shows
Ogden, Iowa   Phone 275-2215

1966 ROUTE

Perry, Iowa	May 9-14
Tama, Iowa	May 16-21
Centerville, Iowa	May 23-28
Denison, Iowa	June 1-4
Belmond, Iowa	June 6-7-8
Janesville, Minn.	June 10-11-12
Fredericksburg, Iowa	June 13-15
Pine Island, Minn.	June 17-18-19
Paynesville, Minn.	June 21-22
Willmar, Minn.	June 23-24-25
Mt. Lake, Minn.	June 27-28
Cannon Falls, Minn.	July 1-2-3-4
Open	July 6-9
Park Rapids, Minn.	July 11-12-13
Detroit Lakes, Minn.	July 14-17
Cambridge, Minn.	July 20-23
Canby, Minn.	July 25-26-27
Henderson, Minn.	July 29-30-31
Grand Meadow, Minn.	Aug. 1-2-3
Osage, Iowa	Aug. 4-7
Preston, Minn.	Aug. 8-11
Waukon, Iowa	Aug. 12-13-14
Algona, Iowa	Aug. 16-19
Seward, Nebr.	Aug. 22-23-24
St. Paul, Nebr.	Aug. 26-27-28
Central City, Nebr.	Aug. 30-31-Sept. 1
Schuyler, Nebr.	Sept. 3-4-5
Waverly, Mo.	Sept. 8-9-10
Piggott, Ark.	Sept. 14-17
Dexter, Mo.	Sept. 19-24
Harrisburg, Ark.	Sept. 27-Oct. 1

Merriam Midway Shows
Ogden, Iowa   Phone 275-2215

1967 ROUTE

Denison, Iowa	May 10-13
Perry, Iowa	May 15-20
Centerville, Iowa	May 22-27
Tama, Iowa	May 29-June 3
Grand Meadow, Minn.	June 5-7
Janesville, Minn.	June 9-11
Fredericksburg, Iowa	June 13-14
Pine Island, Minn.	June 16-17-18
Paynesville, Minn.	June 20-21
Willmar, Minn.	June 22-23-24
Mountain Lake, Minn.	June 26-27
Cannon Falls, Minn.	July 1-4
Park Rapids, Minn.	July 6-9
Detroit Lakes, Minn.	July 11-16
Cambridge, Minn.	July 19-22
Canby, Minn.	July 24-26
Henderson, Minn.	July 28-29-30
Northwood, Iowa	July 31-Aug. 2
Osage, Iowa	Aug. 3-6
Hampton, Iowa	Aug. 7-8-9
Waukon, Iowa	Aug. 10-13
Algona, Iowa	Aug. 15-19
Seward, Nebr.	Aug. 21-22-23
St. Paul, Nebr.	Aug. 25-26-27
Central City, Nebr.	Aug. 29-30-31
Schuyler, Nebr.	Sept. 2-3-4
Carroll, Iowa	Sept. 6-10

Merriam Midway Shows

Ogden, Iowa   Phone 275-2215

1968 ROUTE

Perry, Iowa	May 6-11
Denison, Iowa	May 15-18
Tama, Iowa	May 20-25
Centerville, Iowa	May 27-June 1
Belmond, Iowa	June 3-5
New Hampton, Iowa	June 6-8
Fredericksburg, Iowa	June 11-12
Pine Island, Minn.	June 14-16
Paynesville, Minn.	June 18-19
Willmar, Minn.	June 20-22
Mountain Lake, Minn.	June 24-25
Janesville, Minn.	June 28-30
Cannon Falls, Minn.	July 2-4
Park Rapids, Minn.	July 6-9
Detroit Lakes, Minn.	July 11-14
Cambridge, Minn.	July 17-20
Canby, Minn.	July 22-24
Henderson, Minn.	July 26-28
Olivia, Minn.	July 29-31
Montgomery, Minn.	Aug. 2-4
Northwood, Iowa	Aug. 5-7
Waukon, Iowa	Aug. 8-11
Algona, Iowa	Aug. 13-16
Seward, Nebr.	Aug. 18-21
St. Paul, Nebr.	Aug. 23-25
Central City, Nebr.	Aug. 27-29
Schuyler, Nebr.	Aug. 31-Sept. 2

Merriam Midway Shows

Ogden, Iowa   Phone 515-275-2215

1969 Route

Perry, Iowa	May 5-10
Denison, Iowa	May 14-17
Tama, Iowa	May 19-24
Centerville, Iowa	May 26-31
Belmond, Iowa	June 2-4
Eagle Grove, Iowa	June 6-8
Fredericksburg, Iowa	June 10-11
Pine Island, Minnesota	June 13-15
Paynesville, Minnesota	June 17-18
Willmar, Minnesota	June 19-21
Mountain Lake, Minnesota	June 23-24
Boyd, Minnesota	June 27-29
Cannon Falls, Minnesota	July 2-4
Detroit Lakes, Minnesota	July 8-13
Pequot Lakes, Minnesota	July 14-16
Brooten, Minnesota	July 18-20
Canby, Minnesota	July 22-24
Henderson, Minnesota	July 25-27
Olivia, Minnesota	July 28-30
St. James, Minnesota	July 31-Aug. 3
Northwood, Iowa	August 4-6
Waukon, Iowa	August 7-10
Algona, Iowa	August 12-15
Seward, Nebraska	August 17-20
St. Paul, Nebraska	August 22-24
Central City, Nebraska	August 26-28
Schuyler, Nebraska	August 30-Sept. 1

MERRIAM'S MIDWAY SHOWS

Ogden, Iowa   Phone 515-275-2215

1970 ROUTE

Perry, Iowa	May 4-9
Denison, Iowa	May 13-16
Tama, Iowa	May 18-23
Centerville, Iowa	May 25-30
Belmond, Iowa	June 1-3
Eagle Grove, Iowa	June 5-7
Pocahontas, Iowa	June 11-14
Fredericksburg, Iowa	June 16-17
Red Wing, Minn.	June 19-21
Paynesville, Minn.	June 23-24
Willmar, Minn.	June 25-27
Mountain Lake, Minn.	June 29-30
Cannon Falls, Minn.	July 2-4
Preston, Minn.	July 8-11
Brooten, Minn.	July 13-15
Herman, Minn.	July 16-19
Canby, Minn.	July 21-23
Henderson, Minn.	July 24-26
Olivia, Minn.	July 27-29
St. James, Minn.	July 30 - Aug. 2
Northwood, Iowa	Aug. 3-5
Waukon, Iowa	Aug. 6-9
Algona, Iowa	Aug. 11-14
Sac City, Iowa	Aug. 15-18
Wahoo, Neb.	Aug. 19-22
Seward, Neb.	Aug. 23-26
St. Paul, Neb.	Aug. 28-30
Central City, Neb.	Aug. 31 - Sept. 2
Schuyler, Neb.	Sept. 3-7
Cozad, Neb.	Sept. 11-12

MERRIAM'S MIDWAY SHOWS

Ogden, Iowa   Phone 515-275-2215

1971 ROUTE

Perry, Iowa, Chamber of Commerce	May 3-8
Denison, Iowa, V.F.W.	May 12-15
Tama, Iowa, Fire Department	May 17-22
Centerville, Iowa, Fire Department	May 24-29
Marshalltown, Iowa, Spring Fair	May 31 - June 6
Fredericksburg, Iowa, Celebration	June 8-9
Red Wing, Minn., Y's Mens Carnival	June 11-13
St. Louis Park, Minn., Celebration	June 16-20
Paynesville, Minn., Celebration	June 22-23
Willmar, Minn., Celebration	June 24-26
Mountain Lake, Minn., Celebration	June 28-29
Cannon Falls, Minn., Fair	July 2-4
Fergus Falls, Minn., Fair	July 7-11
Herman, Minn., Fair	July 15-18
Canby, Minn., Fair	July 20-22
Henderson, Minn., Celebration	July 23-25
Olivia, Minn., Celebration	July 26-28
St. James, Minn., Fair	July 29 - Aug. 1
Northwood, Iowa, Fair	Aug. 2-4
Waukon, Iowa, Fair	Aug. 5-8
Algona, Iowa, Fair	Aug. 10-13
Sac City, Iowa, Fair	Aug. 14-17
Albion, Neb., Fair	Aug. 18-21
Seward, Neb., Fair	Aug. 23-25
St. Paul, Neb., Fair	Aug. 27-29
Central City, Neb., Fair	Aug. 30 - Sept. 2
Schuyler, Neb., Celebration	Sept. 5-6
Cozad, Neb., Celebration	Sept. 10-11
Mitchell, S. D., (With Murphy's Shows)	Sept. 19-26

READY TO GO!!!!

1977 ROUTE

Albert Lea, Minnesota 56007...................................May 11-15
    Skyline Mall (Rides only)
Perry, Iowa 50220...May 17-22
    Chamber of Commerce Carnival
Centerville, Iowa 52544......................................May 24-30
    Fire Department Carnival
Tama, Iowa 50339..June 1-5
    Fire Department Carnival
Fredericksburg, Iowa 50630....................................June 7-8
    Dairy Day
Pine Island Minnesota 55963..................................June 10-12
    Cheese Festival
Sherburn, Minnesota 56171...................................June 14-15,
    Holiday Festival
Janesville, Minnesota 56048.................................June 17-19
    Hay Daze Celebration
Paynesville, Minnesota 56362................................June 21-22
    Town and Country Days
Willmar, Minnesota 56201....................................June 23-25
    Kaffe Fest
Mountain Lake, Minnesota 56159..............................June 27-28
    Pow Wow and Barbeque
Cannon Falls, Minnesota 55009.................................July 1-4
    Cannon Valley Fair
Herman, Minnesota 56248......................................July 8-10
    Grant County Fair
Fergus Falls, Minnesota 56537...............................July 13-17
    Otter Tail County Fair
Canby, Minnesota 56220......................................July 19-21
    Yellow Medicine County Fair
Olivia, Minnesota 56277.....................................July 22-24
    Corn Capital Days
Sauk Centre, Minnesota 56378................................July 28-31
    Stearns County Fair
Sanborn, Minnesota 56083.....................................Aug. 2-3
    Watermelon Days
St. James, Minnesota 56081...................................Aug. 4-7
    Watonwan County Fair
Algona, Iowa 50511..Aug. 9-12
    Kossuth County Fair
York, Nebraska 68467.......................................Aug. 15-18
    York County Fair
Seward, Nebraska 68343.....................................Aug. 19-21
    Seward County Fair
Central City, Nebraska 68826...............................Aug. 22-24
    Merrick County Fair
St. Paul, Nebraska 68873...................................Aug. 25-28
    Howard County Fair
Aurora, Nebraska 68818.....................................Aug. 29-31
    Hamilton County Fair
Schuyler, Nebraska 68661....................................Sept. 3-5
    Labor Day Celebration
Madison, Minnesota 56256...................................Sept. 8-11
    Lac Qui Parle County Fair
Open..Sept. 13-16
Mitchell, South Dakota 57301..............................Sept. 18-24
    Corn Palace Festival
    (as Merrian and Baumann Combined Shows)

1977

MAY	1	2	3	4	5	6	7
	8	9	10	11	12	13	14
	15	16	17	18	19	20	21
	22	23	24	25	26	27	28
	29	30	31				

JUNE				1	2	3	4
	5	6	7	8	9	10	11
	12	13	14	15	16	17	18
	19	20	21	22	23	24	25
	26	27	28	29	30		

JUL						1	2
	3	4	5	6	7	8	9
	10	11	12	13	14	15	16
	17	18	19	20	21	22	23
	24	25	26	27	28	29	30
	31						

AUG		1	2	3	4	5	6
	7	8	9	10	11	12	13
	14	15	16	17	18	19	20
	21	22	23	24	25	26	27
	28	29	30	31			

SEP					1	2	3
	4	5	6	7	8	9	10
	11	12	13	14	15	16	17
	18	19	20	21	22	23	24
	25	26	27	28	29	30	

HERE WE COME !!
1 9 7 5   R O U T E

| Perry, Iowa 50220. . . . . May 12-17 |
| Chamber of Commerce Carnival |
| Centerville, Iowa 52544. . . . . . May 19-24 |
| Fire Department Carnival |
| Tama, Iowa 50339 . . . . May 26-31 |
| Fire Department Carnival |
| Belmond, Iowa 50421. . . . . June 2-3-4 |
| Jaycees Street Carnival |
| Pine Island, Minnesota 55963 . . . June 6-7-8 |
| Cheese Festival |
| Fredericksburg, Iowa 50630 . . . . June 10-11 |
| Dairy Day |
| Janesville, Minnesota 56048. . . . June 13-14-15 |
| Hay Daze Celebration |
| Paynesville, Minnesota 56362. . . . June 17-18 |
| Town and Country Days |
| Albert Lea, Minnesota 56007. . . . June 17-21 |
| Skyline Mall (Rides Only) |
| Sherburn, Minnesota 56171 . . . . . June 20-21 |
| Holiday Festival |
| Mountain Lake, Minnesota 56159 . . June 23-24 |
| Pow Wow and Barbeque |
| Willmar, Minnesota 56201 . . . . . June 26-27-28 |
| Kaffe Fest |
| Cannon Falls, Minnesota 55009. . . July 2-3-4 |
| Cannon Valley Fair |
| Fergus Falls, Minnesota 56537. . . July 9-13 |
| Otter Tail County Fair |
| Canby, Minnesota 56220 . . . . . . July 15-16-17 |
| Yellow Medicine County Fair |
| Herman, Minnesota 56248. . . . . . July 18-19-20 |
| Grant County Fair |
| Sauk Centre, Minnesota 56378 . . . July 24-27 |
| Stearns County Fair |
| Sanborn, Minnesota 56083 . . . . . July 29-30 |
| Watermelon Days |
| St. James, Minnesota 56081. . . . July 31-Aug. 3 |
| Watonwan County Fair |
| Algona, Iowa 50511 . . . . Aug. 5-8 |
| Kossuth County Fair |
| Mason City, Iowa 50401. . . . . . Aug. 9-13 |
| North Iowa Fair |
| Seward, Nebraska 68434 . . . . . . Aug. 15-16-17 |
| Seward County Fair |
| Central City, Nebraska 68826. . . Aug. 18-19-20 |
| Merrick County Fair |
| St. Paul, Nebraska 68873. . . . . Aug. 22,23,24 |
| Howard County Fair |
| Aurora, Nebraska 68818. . . . . . Aug. 25,26,27 |
| Hamilton County Fair |
| Schuyler, Nebraska 68661. . . . . Aug. 30-Sept. 1 |
| Labor Day Celebration |
| Cozad, Nebraska 69130 . . . . . . Sept. 5-6 |
| Hay Days |
| Broken Bow, Nebraska 68822. . . . Sept. 10-13 |
| Fall Fest and Hey Days |
| O'Neill, Nebraska 68763 . . . . . Sept. 15-18 |
| Fall Festival |
| Mitchell, South Dakota 57301. . . Sept. 21-27 |
| Corn Palace Festival |
| (as Merriam and Baumann Combined Shows) |

GOING TO BE GREAT !!!!
MERRIAM'S MIDWAY SHOWS, INC.

1978 ROUTE

1978

Albert Lea, Minnesota 56007	May	2 - 5
Skyline Mall (Rides only)		
Perry, Iowa 50220	May	6 -13
Chamber of Commerce Carnival		
Centerville, Iowa 52544	May	15 -20
Fire Department Carnival		
Tama, Iowa 50339	May	24 -29
Fire Department Carnival		
Belmond, Iowa 50421	June	1 - 3
Jaycees Spring Carnival		
Sherburn, Minnesota 56171	June	5 - 7
Centennial Holiday Festival		
Pine Island, Minnesota 55963	June	9 -11
Cheese Festival		
Fredericksburg, Iowa 50630	June 13 -14
Dairy Day		
Janesville, Minnesota 56048	June 16 -18
Hay Daze Celebration		
Paynesville, Minnesota 56362	June 20 -27
Town and Country Days		
Willmar, Minnesota 56201	June 22 -24
Kaffe Fest		
Mountain Lake, Minnesota 56159	June 26 -27
Pow Wow and Barbeque		
Cannon Falls, Minnesota 55009	July 1 - 4
Cannon Valley Fair		
Herman, Minnesota 56248	July 7 - 9
Grant County Fair		
Fergus Falls, Minnesota 56537	July 13 -16
Otter Tail County Fair		
Canby, Minnesota 56220	July 17 -19
Yellow Medicine County Fair		
St. James, Minnesota 56081	July 30 -23
Watonwan County Fair		
Sanborn, Minnesota 56083	July 24 -25
Watermelon Days		
Sauk Centre, Minnesota 56378	July 27 -30
Stearns County Fair		
Anoka, Minnesota 55303	Aug. 1 - 6
Anoka County Suburban Fair		
Algona, Iowa 50511	Aug. 9 -11
Kossuth County Fair		
York, Nebraska 68467	Aug. 14 -17
York County Fair		
Seward, Nebraska 68343	Aug. 18 -20
Seward County Fair		
Central City, Nebraska 68826	Aug. 21 -23
Merrick County Fair		
St. Paul, Nebraska 68873	Aug. 24 -27
Howard County Fair		
Aurora, Nebraska 68818	Aug. 28 -30
Hamilton County Fair		
Schuyler, Nebraska 68661	Sept. 1 - 5
Labor Day Celebration		
Madison, Minnesota 56256	Sept. 7 -10
Lac Qui Parle County Fair		
Mitchell, South Dakota 57301	Sept. 18 -21
Corn Palace Festival		
(as Merriam and Baumann Combined Shows)		

ON THE GO IN '79
MERRIAM'S MIDWAY SHOWS, INC.

1979 ROUTE

1979

Perry, Iowa 50220	May	7 - 12
Chamber of Commerce Carnival		
Centerville, Iowa 52644	May	14 - 19
Fire Department Carnival		
Tama, Iowa 52339	May	23 - 28
Fire Department Carnival		
Belmond, Iowa 50421	May 31 - June 2
Jaycees Spring Carnival		
Sherburn, Minnesota 56171	June	4 - 6
Holiday Festival		
Pine Island, Minnesota 55963	June	8 - 10
Cheese Festival		
Fredericksburg, Iowa 50680	June	12 - 13
Dairy Day		
Janesville, Minnesota 56048	June	15 - 17
Hay Daze Celebration		
Paynesville, Minnesota 56362	June	19 - 20
Town and Country Days		
Willmar, Minnesota 56201	June	21 - 23
Kaffe Fest		
Mountain Lake, Minnesota 56159	June	25 - 26
Pow Wow and Barbeque		
Cannon Falls, Minnesota 55009	July	1 - 4
Cannon Valley Fair		
Herman, Minnesota 56248	July	6 - 8
Grant County Fair		
Fergus Falls, Minnesota 56537	July	11 - 15
Otter Tail County Fair		
Canby, Minnesota 56220	July	16 - 18
Yellow Medicine County Fair		
St. James, Minnesota	July	19 - 22
Watonwan County Fair		
Sanborn, Minnesota 56083	July	23 - 24
Watermelon Days		
Sauk Centre, Minnesota 56378	July	26 - 29
Stearns County Fair		
Anoka, Minnesota 55303	July 31 - Aug. 5
Anoka County Suburban Fair		
Algona, Iowa 50511	Aug.	7 - 10
Kossuth County Fair		
York, Nebraska 68467	Aug.	12 - 16
York County Fair		
Seward, Nebraska 68343	Aug.	17 - 19
Seward County Fair		
Central City, Nebraska 68826	Aug.	20 - 22
Merrick County Fair		
St. Paul, Nebraska 68873	Aug.	23 - 26
Howard County Fair		
Norfolk, Nebraska 68701	Aug.	28 - 31
Sunset Plaza		
Schuyler, Nebraska 68661	Sept.	1 - 5
Labor Day Celebration		
Madison, Minnesota 56256	Sept.	6 - 9
Lac Qui Parle County Fair		
Brookings, South Dakota 57006	Sept.	12 - 16
Harvest Days		
Mitchell, South Dakota 57301	Sept.	23 - 29
Corn Palace Festival		
(as Merriam and Baumann Combined Shows)		

MERRIAM'S MIDWAY SHOWS, INC.

1980 ROUTE

1980

MAY

S	M	T	W	T	F	S
				1	2	3
4	5	6	7	8	9	10
11	12	13	14	15	16	17
18	19	20	21	22	23	24
25	26	27	28	29	30	31

JUNE

S	M	T	W	T	F	S
1	2	3	4	5	6	7
8	9	10	11	12	13	14
15	16	17	18	19	20	21
22	23	24	25	26	27	28
29	30					

JULY

S	M	T	W	T	F	S
		1	2	3	4	5
6	7	8	9	10	11	12
13	14	15	16	17	18	19
20	21	22	23	24	25	26
27	28	29	30	31		

AUGUST

S	M	T	W	T	F	S
					1	2
3	4	5	6	7	8	9
10	11	12	13	14	15	16
17	18	19	20	21	22	23
24	25	26	27	28	29	30

SEPTEMBER

S	M	T	W	T	F	S
	1	2	3	4	5	6
7	8	9	10	11	12	13
14	15	16	17	18	19	20
21	22	23	24	25	26	27
28	29	30				

Perry, Iowa 50220 .... May 12 - 17
 Chamber of Commerce Carnival
Centerville, Iowa 52544 .... May 19 - 24
 Fire Department Carnival
Tama, Iowa 52339 .... May 26 - 31
 Fire Department Carnival
Belmond, Iowa 50421 .... June 2 - 4
 Jaycees Spring Carnival
Pine Island, Minnesota 55963 .... June 6 - 8
 Cheese Festival
Fredericksburg, Iowa 50630 .... June 10 - 11
 Dairy Day
 .... June 13 - 14
Sherburn, Minnesota 56171 .... June 17 - 18
 Holiday Festival
Janesville, Minnesota 56048 .... June 20 - 22
 Hay Daze Celebration
Mountain Lake, Minnesota 56159 .... June 23 - 24
 Pow Wow and Barbeque
Willmar, Minnesota 56201 .... June 26 - 28
 Kaffe Fest
Cannon Falls, Minnesota 55009 .... July 1 - 4
 Cannon Valley Fair
Paynesville, Minnesota 56362 .... July 7 - 9
 Town and Country Days
Herman, Minnesota 56248 .... July 11 - 13
 Grant County Fair
Fergus Falls, Minnesota 56537 .... July 16 - 19
 Otter Tail County Fair
Canby, Minnesota 56220 .... July 21 - 23
 Yellow Medicine County Fair
St. James, Minnesota 56081 .... July 24 - 27
 Watonwan County Fair
Sanborn, Minnesota 56083 .... July 28 - 29
 Watermelon Days
Sauk Centre, Minnesota 56378 .... July 31 - Aug. 3
 Stearns County Fair
Anoka, Minnesota 55303 .... Aug. 5 - 10
 Anoka County Suburban Fair
Algona, Iowa 50511 .... Aug. 12 - 15
 Kossuth County Fair
Fairmont, Minnesota 56031 .... Aug. 16 - 20
 Martin County Fair
St. Paul, Nebraska 68873 .... Aug. 22 - 24
 Howard County Fair
 .... Aug. 25 - 29
Schuyler, Nebraska 68661 .... Aug. 30 - Sept. 1
 Labor Day Celebration
Madison, Minnesota 56256 .... Sept. 4 - 7
 Lac Qui Parle County Fair
Brookings, South Dakota 57006 .... Sept. 10 - 14
 Harvest Days
Mitchell, South Dakota 57031 .... Sept. 21 - 27
 Corn Palace Festival
 (As Merriam and Baumann Combined Shows)

142

MERRIAM'S MIDWAY SHOWS, INC.

1981 ROUTE

1981

MAY
S	M	T	W	T	F	S
					1	2
3	4	5	6	7	8	9
10	11	12	13	14	15	16
17	18	19	20	21	22	23
24	25	26	27	28	29	30
31						

JUNE
S	M	T	W	T	F	S
	1	2	3	4	5	6
7	8	9	10	11	12	13
14	15	16	17	18	19	20
21	22	23	24	25	26	27
28	29	30				

JULY
S	M	T	W	T	F	S
			1	2	3	4
5	6	7	8	9	10	11
12	13	14	15	16	17	18
19	20	21	22	23	24	25
26	27	28	29	30	31	

AUGUST
S	M	T	W	T	F	S
						1
2	3	4	5	6	7	8
9	10	11	12	13	14	15
16	17	18	19	20	21	22
23	24	25	26	27	28	29
30	31					

SEPTEMBER
S	M	T	W	T	F	S
		1	2	3	4	5
6	7	8	9	10	11	12
13	14	15	16	17	18	19
20	21	22	23	24	25	26
27	28	29	30			

Ames, Iowa 50010 .... May 4 - 9
North Grand Mall (Rides Only)

Perry, Iowa 50220 .... May 11 - 16
Chamber of Commerce Carnival

Centerville, Iowa 52544 .... May 18 - 23
Fire Department Carnival

Tama, Iowa 52339 .... May 25 - 30
Fire Department Carnival

Belmond, Iowa 50421 .... June 1 - 3
Jaycees Spring Carnival

Pine Island, Minnesota 55963 .... June 5 - 7
Cheese Festival

Fredericksburg, Iowa 50630 .... June 9 - 10
Dairy Day

Forest City, Iowa 50436 .... June 12 - 14
Frontier Days

Sherburn, Minnesota 56171 .... June 16 - 17
Holiday Festival

Janesville, Minnesota 56048 .... June 19 - 21
Hay Daze Celebration

Willmar, Minnesota 56201 .... June 25 - 27
Kaffe Fest

Mountain Lake, Minnesota 56159 .... June 29 - 30
Pow Wow and Barbeque

Cannon Falls, Minnesota 55009 .... July 2 - 4
Cannon Valley Fair

Paynesville, Minnesota 56362 .... July 6 - 8
Town and Country Days

Herman, Minnesota 56248 .... July 10 - 12
Grant County Fair

Fergus Falls, Minnesota 56537 .... July 15 - 18
Otter Tail County Fair

Canby, Minnesota 56220 .... July 20 - 22
Yellow Medicine County Fair

St. James, Minnesota 56081 .... July 23 - 26
Watonwan County Fair

Sauk Centre, Minnesota 56378 .... July 30 - Aug. 2
Stearns County Fair

Anoka, Minnesota 55303 .... Aug. 4 - 9
Anoka County Suburban Fair

Algona, Iowa 50511 .... Aug. 11 - 14
Kossuth County Fair

Fairmont, Minnesota 56031 .... Aug. 15 - 19
Martin County Fair

St. Paul, Nebraska 68873 .... Aug. 21 - 23
Howard County Fair

Seward, Nebraska 68343 .... Aug. 24 - 26
Seward County Fair

Gothenburg, Nebraska 69138 .... Aug. 28 - 29
Harvest Festival

Schuyler, Nebraska 68661 .... Sept. 5 - 7
Labor Day Celebration

Madison, Minnesota 56256 .... Sept. 10 - 13
Lac Qui Parle County Fair

Brookings, South Dakota 57006 .... Sept. 15 - 18
Harvest Days

Mitchell, South Dakota 57301 .... Sept. 20 - 26
Corn Palace Festival
(As Merriam and Baumann Combined Shows)

MERRIAM'S MIDWAY SHOWS, INC.

1982 ROUTE

Ames, Iowa 50010			May 3 - 8
North Grand Mall (Rides Only)			
Perry, Iowa 50220			May 10 - 15
Chamber of Commerce Carnival			
Tama, Iowa 52339			May 17-22
Fire Department Carnival			
Centerville, Iowa 52544			May 24 - 29
Fire Department Carnival			
Marshalltown, Iowa 50158			May 31 - June 2
Marshalltown Mall			
Forest City, Iowa 50436			June 4 - 6
Frontier Days			
Fredericksburg, Iowa 50630			June 8 - 9
Dairy Day			
Pine Island, Minnesota 55963			June 11 - 13
Cheese Festival			
Sherburn, Minnesota 56171			June 15 - 16
Holiday Festival			
Janesville, Minnesota 56048			June 18 - 20
Hay Daze Celebration			
Willmar, Minnesota 56201			June 25 - 27
Kaffee Fest			
Mountain Lake, Minnesota 56159			June 29 - 30
Pow Wow and Barbeque			
Cannon Falls, Minnesota 55009			July 2 - 4
Cannon Valley Fair			
Paynesville, Minnesota 56362			July 6 - 7
Town and Country Days			
Herman, Minnesota 56248			July 9 - 11
Grant County Fair			
Fergus Falls, Minnesota 56537			July 14 - 17
Otter Tail County Fair			
Canby, Minnesota 56220			July 19 - 21
Yellow Medicine County Fair			
St. James, Minnesota 56081			July 22 - 25
Watonwan County Fair			
Sanborn, Minnesota 56083			July 26 - 27
Watermelon Days			
Sauk Centre, Minnesota 56378			July 29 - Aug. 1
Stearns County Fair			
Anoka, Minnesota 55303			Aug. 3 - 8
Anoka County Suburban Fair			
Algona, Iowa 50511			Aug. 10 -13
Kossuth County Fair			
Fairmont, Minnesota 56031			Aug. 14 - 18
Martin County Fair			
Seward, Nebraska 68343			Aug. 20 - 22
Seward County Fair			
St. Paul, Nebraska 68873			Aug. 26 - 29
Howard County Fair			
O'Neill, Nebraska 68763			Aug. 31 - Sept. 2
Shamrock City Archers Fall Festival			
Schuyler, Nebraska 68661			Sept. 4 - 6
Labor Day Celebration			
Madison, Minnesota 56256			Sept. 9 - 12
Lac Qui Parle County Fair			
Brookings, South Dakota 57006			Sept. 14 - 17
Harvest Days			
Mitchell, South Dakota 57301			Sept. 19 - 26
(As Merriam and Baumann Combined Shows)			

May

S	M	T	W	T	F	S
						1
2	3	4	5	6	7	8
9	10	11	12	13	14	15
16	17	18	19	20	21	22
23	24	25	26	27	28	29
30	31					

June

S	M	T	W	T	F	S
		1	2	3	4	5
6	7	8	9	10	11	12
13	14	15	16	17	18	19
20	21	22	23	24	25	26
27	28	29	30			

July

S	M	T	W	T	F	S
				1	2	3
4	5	6	7	8	9	10
11	12	13	14	15	16	17
18	19	20	21	22	23	24
25	26	27	28	29	30	31

August

S	M	T	W	T	F	S
1	2	3	4	5	6	7
8	9	10	11	12	13	14
15	16	17	18	19	20	21
22	23	24	25	26	27	28
29	30	31				

September

S	M	T	W	T	F	S
			1	2	3	4
5	6	7	8	9	10	11
12	13	14	15	16	17	18
19	20	21	22	23	24	25
26	27	28	29	30		

Fort Dodge, Iowa 50501 .... May 2 - 7
  Crossroads Center (Rides Only)
Perry, Iowa 50220 .... May 9 - 14
  Chamber of Commerce Carnival
Tama, Iowa 52339 .... May 16 - 21
  Fire Department Carnival
Centerville, Iowa 52544 .... May 23 - 28
  Fire Department Carnival
Marshalltown, Iowa 50158 .... May 30 - June 5
  Marshalltown Mall
Fredericksburg, Iowa 60630 .... June 7 - 8
  Dairy Day
Pine Island, Minnesota 55963 .... June 10 - 12
  Cheese Festival
Sanborn, Minnesota 56083 .... June 14 - 16
  Watermelon Days
Janesville, Minnesota 56048 .... June 17 - 19
  Hay Daze Celebration
Willmar, Minnesota 56201 .... June 23 - 25
  Kaffie Fest
Mountain Lake, Minnesota 56159 .... June 27 - 28
  Pow Wow and Barbeque
Cannon Falls, Minnesota 55009 .... July 1 - 4
  Cannon Valley Fair
Paynesville, Minnesota 56362 .... July 6 - 7
  Town and Country Days
Herman, Minnesota 56248 .... July 8 - 10
  Grant County Fair
Fergus Falls, Minnesota 56537 .... July 13 - 16
  Otter Tail County Fair
Canby, Minnesota 56220 .... July 18 - 20
  Yellow Medicine County Fair
St. James, Minnesota 56081 .... July 21 - 24
  Watonwan County Fair
Sauk Centre, Minnesota 56378 .... July 28 - 31
  Stearns County Fair
Anoka, Minnesota 55303 .... Aug. 2 - 7
  Anoka County Suburban Fair
Austin, Minnesota 55912 .... Aug. 8 - 14
  Mower County Fair
Fairmont, Minnesota 56031 .... Aug. 17 - 22
  Martin County Fair
St. Paul, Nebraska 68873 .... Aug. 25 - 28
  Howard County Fair
O'Neill, Nebraska 68763 .... Aug. 30 - Sept. 1
  Shamrock City Archers Fall Festival
Schuyler, Nebraska 68661 .... Sept. 3 - 5
  Labor Day Celebration
Madison, Minnesota 56256 .... Sept. 8 - 11
  Lac Qui Parle County Fair
Brookings, South Dakota 57006 .... Sept. 13 - 16
  Harvest Days
Mitchell, South Dakota 57301 .... Sept. 18 - 24
  Corn Palace

MAY 1983

1	2	3	4	5	6	7
8	9	10	11	12	13	14
15	16	17	18	19	20	21
22	23	24	25	26	27	28
29	30	31				

JUNE 1983

			1	2	3	4
5	6	7	8	9	10	11
12	13	14	15	16	17	18
19	20	21	22	23	24	25
26	27	28	29	30		

JULY 1983

					1	2
3	4	5	6	7	8	9
10	11	12	13	14	15	16
17	18	19	20	21	22	23
24	25	26	27	28	29	30
31						

AUGUST 1983

	1	2	3	4	5	6
7	8	9	10	11	12	13
14	15	16	17	18	19	20
21	22	23	24	25	26	27
28	29	30	31			

SEPTEMBER 1983

				1	2	3
4	5	6	7	8	9	10
11	12	13	14	15	16	17
18	19	20	21	22	23	24
25	26	27	28	29	30	

MERRIAM'S MIDWAY SHOWS, INC.

1984 ROUTE

1984

Location	Handwritten	Date
Fort Dodge, Iowa 50501	—	April 30 - May 5
Crossroads Mall (Rides Only)		
Perry, Iowa 50220	45	May 7 - 12
Chamber of Commerce Carnival		
Tama, Iowa 52339	45	May 14 - 19
Fire Department Carnival		
Centerville, Iowa 52544	45	May 21 - 26
Fire Department Carnival		
Marshalltown, Iowa 50158	45	May 28 - June 3
Marshalltown Mall		
Pine Island, Minnesota 55963	75	June 8 - 10
Cheese Festival		
Fredericksburg, Iowa 50630	25	June 12 - 13
Dairy Days		
Janesville, Minnesota 56048	75	June 15 - 17
Hay Daze Celebration	45	
Paynesville, Minnesota 56362		June 19 - 20
Town and Country Days		
Willmar, Minnesota 56201	75	June 21 - 23
Kaffee Fest	45	
Mountain Lake, Minnesota 56159		June 25 - 26
Pow Wow and Barbeque	45	
Eden Valley, Minnesota 55329		June 28 - 30
Valley Daze		
Cannon Falls, Minnesota 55009	175	July 1 - 4
Cannon Valley Fair	45	
Sanborn, Minnesota 56083		July 6 - 7
Watermelon Days	45	
Norfolk, Nebraska 68701		July 10 - 15
Sunset Plaza		
Columbus, Nebraska 68601	125	July 18 - 22
Platte County Fair		
Sioux City, Iowa 51100	25/F.T.	July 25 - 29
Rivercade		
Anoka, Minnesota 55303	250	July 31 - Aug. 5
Anoka County Suburban Fair	10/F.T.	
Austin, Minnesota 55912		Aug. 6 - 12
Mower County Fair		
Fairmont, Minnesota 56031	125	Aug. 15 - 20
Martin County Fair		
Fergus Falls, Minnesota 56537	175	Aug. 22 - 25
Otter Tail County Fair		
Brookings, South Dakota 57006	15	Aug. 27 - 29
Harvest Days		
Winner, South Dakota 57580	75	Aug. 31 - Sept. 3
Labor Day Celebration		
Cozad, Nebraska 60130	75	Sept. 7 - 8
Hay Days	45	
Broken Bow, Nebraska 68822		Sept. 10 - 12
Jaycees Fall Carnival		
Gothenburg, Nebraska 69138	75	Sept. 13 - 15
Harvest Festival	45	
O'Neill, Nebraska 68763		Sept. 17 - 19
Shamrock City Archers Fall Festival	45	
Butte, Nebraska 68722		Sept. 20 - 21
Pancake Days		
Mitchell, South Dakota 57301	125/F.T.	Sept. 23 - 29
Corn Palace		

146

MERRIAM'S MIDWAY SHOWS, INC.

1985 ROUTE

```
Fort Dodge, Iowa 50501 . . . . . . . . . . . . . . . . May 6 - 11
    Crossroads Mall (Rides Only)
Marshalltown, Iowa 50158 . . . . . . . . . . . . . May 13 - 18
    Marshalltown Mall
Centerville, Iowa 52544 . . . . . . . . . . . . . May 20 - 25
    Fire Department Carnival
Tama, Iowa 52339 . . . . . . . . . . . . . . May 29 - June 1
    Fire Department Carnival
Belmond, Iowa 52544 . . . . . . . . . . . . . . June 3 - 5
    Jaycees Spring Carnival
Pine Island, Minnesota 55963 . . . . . . . . . . June 7 - 9
    Cheese Festival
Fredericksburg, Iowa 50630 . . . . . . . . . . June 11 - 12
    Dairy Days
Janesville, Minnesota 56048 . . . . . . . . . June 14 - 16
    May Daze Celebration
Paynesville, Minnesota 56362 . . . . . . . . . June 18 - 19
    Town and Country Days
Mountain Lake, Minnesota 56159 . . . . . . . . June 24 - 25
    Pow Wow and Barbeque
Willmar, Minnesota 56201 . . . . . . . . . . . June 27 - 29
    Kaffee Fest
Cannon Falls, Minnesota 55009 . . . . . . . . . July 1 - 4
    Cannon Valley Fair
Sanborn, Minnesota 56083 . . . . . . . . . . . July 6 - 7
    Watermelon Days
Columbus, Nebraska 68601 . . . . . . . . . . . July 10 - 14
    Platte County Fair
Norfolk, Nebraska 68701 . . . . . . . . . . . July 16 - 21
    Sunset Plaza
Sioux City, Iowa 51100 . . . . . . . . . . . . July 25 - 28
    Rivercade
Anoka, Minnesota 55303 . . . . . . . . . July 30 - Aug. 4
    Anoka County Suburban Fair
Austin, Minnesota 55912 . . . . . . . . . . Aug. 6 - 11
    Mower County Fair
Fairmont, Minnesota 56031 . . . . . . . . . Aug. 13 - 18
    Martin County Fair
Fergus Falls, Minnesota 56537 . . . . . . . Aug. 21 - 24
    Otter Tail County Fair
Brookings, South Dakota 57006 . . . . . . . Aug. 26 - 29
    Harvest Days
Winner, South Dakota 57580 . . . . . . Aug. 31 - Sept. 2
    Labor Day Celebration
Cozad, Nebraska 60130 . . . . . . . . . . . Sept. 6 - 7
    Hay Days
O'Neill, Nebraska 68763 . . . . . . . . . . Sept. 9 - 11
    Shamrock City Archers Fall Festival
Butte, Nebraska 68722 . . . . . . . . . . . Sept. 12 - 13
    Pancake Days
Mitchell, South Dakota 57301 . . . . . . . Sept. 15 - 22
    Corn Palace
```

MERRIAM'S MIDWAY SHOWS, INC

1986 ROUTE

```
Fort Dodge, Iowa 50501 . . . . . . . . . . . . . . . . May 5 - 10
    Crossroads Mall (Rides Only)
Marshalltown, Iowa 50158 . . . . . . . . . . . . . May 12 - 17
    Marshalltown Mall
Centerville, Iowa 52544 . . . . . . . . . . . . . May 19 - 24
    Fire Department Carnival
Tama, Iowa 52339 . . . . . . . . . . . . . . . May 28 - 31
    Fire Department Carnival
Belmond, Iowa 52544 . . . . . . . . . . . . . . June 2 - 4
    Jaycees Spring Carnival
Pine Island, Minnesota 55963 . . . . . . . . . June 6 - 8
    Cheese Festival
Fredericksburg, Iowa 50630 . . . . . . . . . . June 10 - 11
    Dairy Days
Janesville, Minnesota 56048 . . . . . . . . . June 13 - 15
    Hay Days
Paynesville, Minnesota 56362 . . . . . . . . . June 17 - 19
    Town and Country Days
Merrill, Iowa 51038 . . . . . . . . . . . . . June 19 - 21
    Town and Country Days
Mountain Lake, Minnesota 56159 . . . . . . . . June 23 - 24
    Pow Wow and Barbeque
Willmar, Minnesota 56201 . . . . . . . . . . . June 26 - 28
    Kaffe Fest
Lake City, Minnesota 55041 . . . . . . . . . . June 27 - 29
    Water Ski Days
Cannon Falls, Minnesota 55009 . . . . . . . . . July 1 - 4
    Cannon Valley Fair
Columbus, Nebraska 68601 . . . . . . . . . . . July 9 - 13
    Platte County Fair
Norfolk, Nebraska 68701 . . . . . . . . . . . July 15 - 20
    Sunset Plaza
Sioux City, Iowa 51100 . . . . . . . . . . . . July 23 - 27
    Rivercade
Anoka, Minnesota 55303 . . . . . . . . . July 29 - Aug. 3
    Anoka County Suburban Fair
Austin, Minnesota 55912 . . . . . . . . . . Aug. 5 - 10
    Mower County Fair
Fairmont, Minnesota 56031 . . . . . . . . . Aug. 12 - 17
    Martin County Fair
Fergus Falls, Minnesota 56537 . . . . . . . Aug. 20 - 23
    Otter Tail County Fair
Sanborn, Minnesota 56083 . . . . . . . . . Aug. 25 - 26
    Watermelon Days
Winner, South Dakota 57580 . . . . . . Aug. 30 - Sept. 1
    Labor Day Celebration
Cozad, Nebraska 60130 . . . . . . . . . . . Sept. 5 - 6
    Hay Days
O'Neill, Nebraska 68763 . . . . . . . . . . Sept. 8 - 10
    Shamrock City Archers Fall Festival
Mitchell, South Dakota 57301 . . . . . . . Sept. 13 - 21
    Corn Palace
```

147

Fort Dodge, Iowa 50501 . . . . May 4 - 9
    Crossroads Mall (Rides Only)
Marshalltown, Iowa 50158 . . . . May 11 - 16
    Marshalltown Mall
Centerville, Iowa 52544 . . . . May 18 - 23
    Fire Department Carnival
Tama, Iowa 52339 . . . . May 27 - 30
    Fire Department Carnival
Belmond, Iowa 52544 . . . . June 1 - 3
    Jaycees Spring Carnival
Pine Island, Minnesota 55963 . . . . June 5 - 7
    Cheese Festival
Fredericksburg, Iowa 50630 . . . . June 9 - 10
    Dairy Days
Merrill, Iowa 51038 . . . . June 12 - 13
    Town and Country Days
South Sioux City, Nebraska 68776 . . . . . . June 13 - 20
    Centennial (With Evans United Shows)
Paynesville, Minnesota 56362 . . . . June 16 - 17
    Town and Country Days
Janesville, Minnesota 56048 . . . . June 19 - 21
    Hay Days
Mountain Lake, Minnesota 56159 . . . . June 22 - 23
    Pow Wow and Barbeque
Lake City, Minnesota 55041 . . . . June 26 - 28
    Water Ski Days
Cannon Falls, Minnesota 55009 . . . . July 1 - 4
    Cannon Valley Fair
Columbus, Nebraska 68601 . . . . July 8 - 12
    Platte County Fair
Faribault, Minnesota 55021 . . . . July 14 - 19
    Rice County Fair
Sioux City, Iowa 51100 . . . . July 22 - 26
    Rivercade
Sanborn, Minnesota 56083 . . . . July 28 - 29
    Watermelon Days
Redwood Falls, Minnesota 56283 . . . . . July 30 - Aug. 2
    Redwood County Fair
Anoka, Minnesota 55303 . . . . Aug. 4 - 9
    Anoka County Suburban Fair
Austin, Minnesota 55912 . . . . Aug. 11 - 16
    Mower County Fair
Fairmont, Minnesota 56031 . . . . Aug. 18 - 25
    Martin County Fair
Fergus Falls, Minnesota 56537 . . . . Aug. 26 - 29
    Otter Tail County Fair
Independence, Missouri 64050 . . . . Sept. 3 - 7
    Labor Day Celebration (With Dillard Shows)
Winner, South Dakota 57580 . . . . Sept. 5 - 7
    Labor Day Celebration
Cozad, Nebraska 60130 . . . . Sept. 11 - 12
    Hay Days (With D. C. Lynch Shows)
Mitchell, South Dakota 57301 . . . . Sept. 12 - 20
    Corn Palace

MERRIAM'S MIDWAY SHOWS, INC.

1988 ROUTE (AS OF 4/21/88)

Fairmont, Minnesota 56031 . (White Unit) April 29 - May 1
    Fairmall Spring Carnival
Fort Dodge, Iowa 50501 . . NONE . . . . May 9 - 14
    Crossroads Mall (Rides Only)
Centerville, Iowa 52544 515-856-2805. . May 16 - 21
    Fire Department Carnival
Tama, Iowa 52339 . . 515-484-3011 . . . . . May 23 - 28
    Fire Department Carnival
Marshalltown, Iowa 50158 . 515-752-7224. May 30 - June 4
    Marshalltown Mall
Fredericksburg, Iowa 50630 319-237-6272. June 7 - 8
    Dairy Days
Pine Island, Minnesota 55963 507-356-8788 June 10 - 12
    Cheese Festival   612-243-3780
Paynesville, Minnesota 56362 . (Red Unit) . June 14 - 15
    Town and Country Days 507-234-6202
Janesville, Minnesota 56048 (Red Unit) . June 17 - 19
    Hay Days
Lake City, Minnesota 55041 612-345-5693 . June 24 - 26
    Water Ski Days   507-662-6639
Lakefield, Minnesota 56151 . (Blue Unit) . June 16 - 18
    Summerfest '88
Belmond, Iowa 50421 . . NONE (Blue Unit) . June 23 - 25
    Jaycee Spring Carnival
Mountain Lake, Minnesota 56159 (Blue Unit) . June 27 - 28 NONE
    Pow Wow and Barbeque
Cannon Falls, Minnesota 55009 507-263-5451 July 1 - 4
    Cannon Valley Fair
Columbus, Nebraska 68601 . 402-563-3690. July 6 - 10
    Platte County Fair
Sanborn, Minnesota 56083 . . NONE. . . . . July 12 - 13
    Watermelon Days
Redwood Falls, Minnesota 56283 507-637-3128 July 14 - 17
    Redwood County Fair
Faribault, Minnesota 55021 . 507-334-2698 July 19 - 24
    Rice County Fair
Sioux City, Iowa 51100 . 712-277-1630 . . July 27 - 31
    Rivercade
Anoka, Minnesota 55303 . 612-427-0135 . . . . Aug. 2 - 7
    Anoka County Suburban Fair
Austin, Minnesota 55912 . . 507-433-9070 Aug. 9 - 14
    Mower County Fair
Fairmont, Minnesota 56031 507-235-2698. Aug. 16 - 21
    Martin County Fair
Fergus Falls, Minnesota 56537 218-736-3891 Aug. 24 - 27
    Otter Tail County Fair
Winner, South Dakota 57580 . 605-842-3650. Sept. 3 - 5
    Labor Day Celebration
Mitchell, South Dakota 57301 605-996-5261 sept. 10 - 18
    Corn Palace

MERRIAM'S MIDWAY SHOWS, INC.

1969 ROUTE

Fort Dodge, Iowa 50501 . . . . *NONE* . . . . . May 6 - 13
   Crossroads Mall (Rides Only)
Tama, Iowa 52339   *515-484-3011* . . . . . . May 17 - 20
   Fire Department Carnival
Centerville, Iowa 52544   *515-856-2205* . . May 22 - 27
   Fire Department Carnival
Marshalltown, Iowa 50158 . *515-752-4516* May 29 - June 3
   Marshalltown Mall
Belmond, Iowa 50421   *515-444-9296* . June 5 - 7.
   Jaycees Spring Carnival
Pine Island, Minnesota 55963 *507-356-8788* June 9 - 11
   Cheese Festival
Fredericksburg, Iowa 50630 *319-237-6272* June 13 - 14
   Dairy Days
Janesville, Minnesota 56048 *507-234-6202* June 16 - 18
   Hay Days
Paynesville, Minnesota 56362 *612-243-3780* June 20 - 21
   Town and Country Days
Sherburn, Minnesota 56171 . *NONE* . . . June 22 - 25
   Holiday Festival
Lake City, Minnesota 55041 *612-345-5540* June 23 - 25
   Water Ski Days
Mountain Lake, Minnesota 56159 *507-427-2981* June 26 - 27
   Pow Wow and Barbeque
Cannon Falls, Minnesota 55009 *507-263-4434* June 30 - July 4
   Cannon Valley Fair
Columbus, Nebraska 68601 *402-563-3640* . . July 6 - 9
   Platte County Fair
Sanborn, Minnesota 56083 *507-648-3442* . July 11 - 12
   Watermelon Days
Redwood Falls, Minnesota 56283 *507-637-3728* July 13 - 16
   Redwood County Fair
Faribault, Minnesota 55021 . *507-332-2629* July 18 - 23
   Rice County Fair
Sioux City, Iowa 51100 *712-258-3435* . July 26 - 30
   Rivercade
Anoka, Minnesota 55303 . *612-422-2096* . . Aug. 1 - 6
   Anoka County Suburban Fair
Austin, Minnesota 55912 . *507-433-2197* . . Aug 8 - 13
   Mower County Fair
Fairmont, Minnesota 56031 *507-238-2808* . Aug. 15 - 20
   Martin County Fair
Winner, South Dakota 57580 *605-842-3656* . Sept. 2 - 4
   Labor Day Celebration
Mitchell, South Dakota 57301 *605-996-5261* Sept. 14 - 17
   Corn Palace

NORFOLK, NEBRASKA   402-379-2514   Aug 25 - Aug 30

MINN STATE FAIR   612-643-0311

MERRIAM'S MIDWAY SHOWS, INC.
TEMPE, ARIZONA
1991 ROUTE (BLUE UNIT)

Fairmont, Minnesota 56031 . . . . May 1 - 4
   Fair Mall Spring Carnival (Blue Unit)
Fort Dodge, Iowa 50501 . . . . May 8 - 11
   Crossroads Mall (Combined Units, Rides Only)
Chariton, Iowa 50049 . . . . May 15 - 16
   Downtown Spring Carnival (Blue Unit)
Perry, Iowa 50220 . . . . May 20 - 25
   Chamber of Commerce Spring Carnival (Blue Unit)
Worthington, Minnesota . . . . May 27 - 29
   Northland Mall Spring Carnival (Blue Unit)
Sisseton, South Dakota 57262 . . . . May 31 - June 2
   F.A.N. Club Carnival (Blue Unit)
Brookings, South Dakota . . . . June 4 - 8
   University Mall Spring Fling (Blue Unit)
Watertown, South Dakota 57201 . . . . . . June 7 - 12
   Watertown Mall (Blue Unit)
Janesville, Minnesota 56048 . . . . June 14 - 16
   Hay Days (Blue Unit)
Paynesville, Minnesota 56362 . . . . June 18 - 19
   Town and Country Days (Blue Unit)
Aberdeen, South Dakota 57401 . . . . June 21 - 23
   Storybook Land (Blue Unit)
Norfolk, Nebraska 68701 . . . . June 25 - 27
   Sunset Plaza Giant Spring Carnival (Blue Unit)
Blair, Nebraska 68008 . . . . June 28 - 30
   Gateway to the West Celebration (Blue Unit)
Columbus, Nebraska 68601 . . . . July 3 - 7
   Platte County Fair (Combined Units)
Sanborn, Minnesota 56083 . . . . July 9 - 10
   Watermelon Days (Blue Unit)
Pending . . . . July 11 - 14
   (Blue Unit)
Faribault, Minnesota 55021 . . . . July 16 - 21
   Rice County Fair (Combined Units)
Sioux City, Iowa 51100 . . . . July 24 - 28
   Rivercade (Combined Units)
Anoka, Minnesota 55303 . . . . . . July 30 - Aug. 4
   Anoka County Fair (Combined Units)
Austin, Minnesota 55912 . . . . Aug. 6 - 11
   Mower County Fair (Combined Units)
Fairmont, Minnesota 56031 . . . . Aug. 13 - 18
   Martin County Fair (Combined Units)
Fergus Falls, Minnesota 56537 . . . . . . Aug. 21 - 24
   Otter Tail County Fair (Combined Units)
Brookings, South Dakota 57580 . . . . . . Aug. 26 - 29
   Harvest Days (Combined Units)
Winner, South Dakota 57580 . . . . . Aug. 31 - Sept. 3
   Labor Day Celebration (Combined Units)
Mitchell, South Dakota 57301 . . . . . . Sept. 7 - 15
   Corn Palace (Combined Units)

149

Fort Dodge, Iowa 50501 . . . . May 6 - 11
    Crossroads Mall (Combined Units, Rides Only)
Tama, Iowa 52339 . . . . May 15 - 18
    Fire Dept. Carnival (Red Unit)
Centerville, Iowa 52544 . . . . May 20 - 25
    Fire Dept. Carnival (Red Unit)
Marshalltown, Iowa 50158 . . . . May 27 - June 1
    Marshalltown Mall (Red Unit)
Belmond, Iowa 50421 . . . . June 3 - 5
    Jaycees Spring Carnival (Red Unit)
Pine Island, Minnesota 55963 . . . . June 7 - 9
    Cheese Festival (Red Unit)
Fredericksburg, Iowa 50630 . . . . June 11 - 12
    Dairy Days (Red Unit)
State Center, Iowa 50247 . . . . June 14 - 16
    Rose Festival (Red Unit)
Albert Lea, Minnesota . . . . June 18 - 20
    Skyline Mall Carnival Days (Red Unit)
Sherburn, Minnesota 56171 . . . . June 21 - 23
    Holiday Festival (Red Unit)
Mountain Lake, Minnesota 56159 . . . . June 24 - 25
    Pow Wow and Barbeque (Red Unit)
Lake City, Minnesota 55041 . . . . June 28 - 30
    Water Ski Days (Red Unit)
Columbus, Nebraska 68601 . . . . July 3 - 7
    Platte County Fair (Combined Units)
Redwood Falls, Minnesota 56283 . . . . July 11 - 14
    Redwood County Fair (Red Unit)
Faribault, Minnesota 55021 . . . . July 18 - 21
    Rice County Fair (Combined Units)
Sioux City, Iowa 51100 . . . . July 24 - 28
    Rivercade (Combined Units)
Anoka, Minnesota 55303 . . . . July 30 - Aug. 4
    Anoka County Fair (Combined Units)
Austin, Minnesota 55912 . . . . Aug. 6 - 11
    Mower County Fair (Combined Units)
Fairmont, Minnesota 56031 . . . . Aug. 13 - 18
    Martin County Fair (Combined Units)
Fergus Falls, Minnesota 56537 . . . . Aug. 21 - 24
    Otter Tail County Fair (Combined Units)
Brookings, South Dakota 57580 . . . . Aug. 26 - 29
    Harvest Days (Combined Units)
Winner, South Dakota 57580 . . . . . . Aug. 31 - Sept. 2
    Labor Day Celebration (Combined Units)
Mitchell, South Dakota 57301 . . . . Sept. 7 - 15
    Corn Palace (Combined Units)

Fairmont, Minnesota 56031 . . . . April 29 - May 2
    Fair Mall Spring Carnival (Blue Unit)
Fort Dodge, Iowa 50501 . . . . May 4 - 9
    Crossroads Mall (Combined Units, Rides Only)
Perry, Iowa 50220 . . . . May 11 - 16
    Chamber of Commerce Spring Carnival (Blue Unit)
Worthington, Minnesota . . . . May 18 - 20
    Northland Mall Spring Carnival (Blue Unit)
Okoboji, Iowa 51355 . . . . May 21 - 25
    Memorial Day by the Lake Days (Blue Unit)
Omaha, Nebraska . . . . May 27 - 31
    Sports Plaza (Blue Unit)
Norfolk, Nebraska 68701 . . . . June 3 - 7
    Sunset Plaza Giant Spring Carnival (Blue Unit)
Watertown, South Dakota 57201 . . . . June 10 - 14
    Watertown Mall (Blue Unit)
Paynesville, Minnesota 56362 . . . . June 16 - 17
    Town and Country Days (Blue Unit)
Janesville, Minnesota 56048 . . . . June 19 - 21
    Hay Days (Blue Unit)
Barnesville, Minnesota 56514 . . . . June 24 - 27
    Clay County Fair (Blue Unit)
Bemidji, Minnesota 56601 . . . . July 1 - 5
    Jaycees Water Carnival (Combined Units)
Sanborn, Minnesota 56083 . . . . July 7 - 8
    Watermelon Days (Blue Unit)
Redwood Falls, Minnesota 56283 . . . . July 9 - 12
    Redwood County Fair (Blue Unit)
Columbus, Nebraska 68601 . . . . July 15 - 19
    Platte County Fair (Combined Units)
Sioux City, Iowa 51100 . . . . July 21 - 26
    Rivercade (Combined Units)
Faribault, Minnesota 55021 . . . . July 28 - Aug. 2
    Rice County Fair (Combined Units)
Anoka, Minnesota 55303 . . . . Aug. 4 - 9
    Anoka County Fair (Combined Units)
Austin, Minnesota 55912 . . . . Aug. 11 - 16
    Mower County Fair (Combined Units)
Fairmont, Minnesota 56031 . . . . Aug. 18 - 23
    Martin County Fair (Combined Units)
Fergus Falls, Minnesota 56537 . . . . Aug. 26 - 29
    Otter Tail County Fair (Combined Units)
Pending . . . . Aug. 31 - Sept. 3
    (Combined Units)
Winner, South Dakota 57580 . . . . Sept. 5 - 7
    Labor Day Celebration (Combined Units)
Mitchell, South Dakota 57301 . . . . Sept. 12 - 20
    Corn Palace (Combined Units)

MERRIAM'S MIDWAY SHOWS, INC.
TEMPE, ARIZONA

1992 ROUTE (RED UNIT)

Fort Dodge, Iowa 50501 . . . . May 4 - 9
    Crossroads Mall (Combined Units, Rides Only)
Tama, Iowa 52339 . . . . May 13 - 16
    Fire Dept. Carnival (Red Unit)
Centerville, Iowa 52544 . . . . May 18 - 23
    Fire Dept. Carnival (Red Unit)
Marshalltown, Iowa 50158 . . . . May 25 - 30
    Marshalltown Mall (Red Unit)
Belmond, Iowa 50421 . . . . June 1 - 3
    Jaycees Spring Carnival (Red Unit)
Algona, Iowa 50511 . . . . June 5 - 7
    Chamber of Commerce Spring Carnival (Red Unit)
Fredericksburg, Iowa 50630 . . . . June 9 - 10
    Dairy Days (Red Unit)
Pine Island, Minnesota 55963 . . . . June 12 - 14
    Cheese Festival (Red Unit)
Blair Nebraska 68008 . . . . June 18 - 20
    Gateway to the West Celebration (Red Unit)
Mountain Lake, Minnesota 56159 . . . . June 22 - 23
    Pow Wow and Barbeque (Red Unit)
Lake City, Minnesota 55041 . . . . June 26 - 28
    Water Ski Days (Red Unit)
Bemidji, Minnesota 56601 . . . . July 1 - 5
    Jaycees Water Carnival (Combined Units)
St. Charles, Minnesota 55972 . . . . July 8 - 12
    Winona County Fair (Red Unit)
Columbus, Nebraska 68601 . . . . July 15 - 19
    Platte County Fair (Combined Units)
Sioux City, Iowa 51100 . . . . July 21 - 26
    Rivercade (Combined Units)
Faribault, Minnesota 55021 . . . . July 28 - Aug. 2
    Rice County Fair (Combined Units)
Anoka, Minnesota 55303 . . . . Aug. 4 - 9
    Anoka County Fair (Combined Units)
Austin, Minnesota 55912 . . . . Aug. 11 - 16
    Mower County Fair (Combined Units)
Fairmont, Minnesota 56031 . . . . Aug. 18 - 23
    Martin County Fair (Combined Units)
Fergus Falls, Minnesota 56537 . . . . Aug. 26 - 29
    Otter Tail County Fair (Combined Units)
Pending . . . . Aug. 31 - Sept. 3
    (Combined Units)
Winner, South Dakota 57580 . . . . Sept. 5 - 7
    Labor Day Celebration (Combined Units)
Mitchell, South Dakota 57301 . . . . Sept. 12 - 20
    Corn Palace (Combined Units)

MERRIAM'S MIDWAY SHOWS, INC.
TEMPE, ARIZONA

1993 ROUTE (BLUE UNIT)

Fort Dodge, Iowa 50501 . . . . May 3 - 9
    Crossroads Mall (Combined Units, Rides Only)
Perry, Iowa 50220 . . . . May 10 - 15
    Chamber of Commerce Spring Carnival (Blue Unit)
Centerville, Iowa 52544 . . . . May 17 - 22
    Fire Department Spring Carnival (Blue Unit)
Marshalltown, Iowa 50158 . . . . May 24 - 29
    Marshall Town Center (Blue Unit)
Norfolk, Nebraska 68701 . . . . June 2 - 6
    Sunset Plaza Giant Spring Carnival (Blue Unit)
Blair, Nebraska 68008 . . . . June 10 - 12
    Gateway to the West Celebration (Blue Unit)
North Platte, Nebraska 6910 . . . . June 15 - 20
    Nebraskaland Days (Blue Unit)
Barnesville, Minnesota 56514 . . . . June 23 - 26
    Clay County Fair (Blue Unit)
Ada, Minnesota 56510 . . . . June 27 - 30
    Norman County Fair (Blue Unit)
Bemidji, Minnesota 56601 . . . . July 1 - 5
    Jaycees Water Carnival (Blue Unit)
Redwood Falls, Minnesota 56283 . . . . July 8 - 11
    Redwood County Fair (Blue Unit)
Columbus, Nebraska 68601 . . . . July 14 - 18
    Platte County Fair (Combined Units)
Sioux City, Iowa 51100 . . . . July 20 - 25
    Rivercade (Combined Units)
Faribault, Minnesota 55021 . . . . July 27 - Aug. 1
    Rice County Fair (Combined Units)
Anoka, Minnesota 55303 . . . . Aug. 3 - 8
    Anoka County Fair (Combined Units)
Austin, Minnesota 55912 . . . . Aug. 10 - 15
    Mower County Fair (Combined Units)
New Ulm, Minnesota 56073 . . . . Aug. 18 - 22
    Brown County Fair (Blue Unit)
Fergus Falls, Minnesota 56537 . . . . Aug. 25 - 28
    Otter Tail County Fair (Combined Units)
Pierre, South Dakota 57501 . . . . Sept. 9 - 12
    Pierre Mall (Combined Units)
Mitchell, South Dakota 57301 . . . . Sept. 16 - 26
    Corn Palace (Combined Units)

1993 ROUTE (RED UNIT)

Fairmont, Minnesota 56031 . . . . April 28 - May 1
    Fairmall Spring Carnival (Red Unit)
Fort Dodge, Iowa 50501 . . . . May 3 - 8
    Crossroads Mall (Combined Units, Rides Only)
Tama, Iowa 52339 . . . . May 12 - 15
    Fire Dept. Carnival (Red Unit)
Ames, Iowa 50010 . . . . May 17 - 22
    North Grand Mall (Red Unit)
Spencer, Iowa 50301 . . . . May 24 - 27
    Southpark Mall (Red Unit)
Okoboji, Iowa . . . . May 28 - 30
    Memorial Day by the Lake Days (Red Unit)
Belmond, Iowa 50421 . . . . May 31 - June 2
    Jaycees Spring Carnival (Red Unit)
Mason City, Iowa 50401 . . . . June 4 - 6
    State Band Festival (Red Unit)
Fredericksburg, Iowa 50630 . . . . June 8 - 9
    Dairy Days (Red Unit)
Pine Island, Minnesota 55963 . . . . June 11 - 13
    Cheese Festival (Red Unit)
Paynesville, Minnesota 56362 . . . . June 15 - 16
    Town and Country Days (Red Unit)
Janesville Minnesota 56048 . . . . June 18 - 20
    Hay Days (Red Unit)
Mountain Lake, Minnesota 56159 . . . . June 21 - 22
    Pow Wow and Barbeque (Red Unit)
Lake City, Minnesota 55041 . . . . June 25 - 27
    Water Ski Days (Red Unit)
Shell Rock, Iowa 50670 . . . . July 1 - 4
    4th of July Celebration (Red Unit)
St. Charles, Minnesota 55972 . . . . July 7 - 11
    Winona County Fair (Red Unit)
Columbus, Nebraska 68601 . . . . July 14 - 18
    Platte County Fair (Combined Units)
Sioux City, Iowa 51100 . . . . July 20 - 25
    Rivercade (Combined Units)
Faribault, Minnesota 55021 . . . . July 27 - Aug. 1
    Rice County Fair (Combined Units)
Anoka, Minnesota 55303 . . . . Aug. 3 - 8
    Anoka County Fair (Combined Units)
Austin, Minnesota 55912 . . . . Aug. 10 - 15
    Mower County Fair (Combined Units)
Fairmont, Minnesota 56031 . . . . Aug. 17 - 22
    Martin County Fair (Red Unit)
Fergus Falls, Minnesota 56537 . . . . Aug. 25 - 28
    Otter Tail County Fair (Combined Units)
Brookings, South Dakota 57580 . . . . . Aug. 30 - Sept. 2
    Harvest Days (Red Unit)
Winner, South Dakota 57580 . . . . Sept. 4 - 6
    Labor Day Celebration (Red Unit)
Pierre, South Dakota 57501 . . . . Sept. 9 - 12
    Pierre Mall (Combined Units)
Mitchell, South Dakota 57301 . . . . Sept. 16 - 26
    Corn Palace (Combined Units)

1994 ROUTE (BLUE UNIT)

Fort Dodge, Iowa 50501 . . . . May 9 - 14
    Crossroads Mall (Combined Units, Rides Only)
Perry, Iowa 50220 . . . . May 16 - 21
    Chamber of Commerce Spring Carnival (Blue Unit)
Marshalltown, Iowa 50158 . . . . May 23 - 28
    Marshall Town Center (Blue Unit)
Norfolk, Nebraska 68701 . . . . June 1 - 5
    Sunset Plaza Giant Spring Carnival (Blue Unit)
Blair, Nebraska 68008 . . . . June 9 - 11
    Gateway to the West Celebration (Blue Unit)
North Platte, Nebraska 69103 . . . . June 14 - 20
    Nebraskaland Days (Blue Unit)
Barnesville, Minnesota 56514 . . . . June 23 - 26
    Clay County Fair (Blue Unit)
Ada, Minnesota 56510 . . . . June 27 - 29
    Norman County Fair (Blue Unit)
Bemidji, Minnesota 56601 . . . . June 30 - July 4
    Jaycees Water Carnival (Blue Unit)
Redwood Falls, Minnesota 56283 . . . . July 7 - 10
    Redwood County Fair (Blue Unit)
Columbus, Nebraska 68601 . . . . July 13 - 17
    Platte County Fair (Combined Units)
Faribault, Minnesota 55021 . . . . July 19 - 24
    Rice County Fair (Combined Units)
Sioux City, Iowa 51100 . . . . July 26 - 31
    Rivercade (Combined Units)
Anoka, Minnesota 55303 . . . . Aug. 2 - 7
    Anoka County Fair (Combined Units)
Austin, Minnesota 55912 . . . . Aug. 9 - 14
    Mower County Fair (Combined Units)
Owatonna, Minnesota 55060 . . . . Aug. 16 - 21
    Steele County Fair (Combined Units)
Fergus Falls, Minnesota 56537 . . . . Aug. 24 - 27
    Otter Tail County Fair (Combined Units)
Omaha, Nebraska 68131 . . . . Sept. 1 - 5
    Septemberfest (Combined Units)
Mitchell, South Dakota 57301 . . . . Sept. 10 - 18
    Corn Palace (Combined Units)

152

MERRIAM'S MIDWAY SHOWS, INC.
TEMPE, ARIZONA

1994 ROUTE (RED UNIT)

Fort Dodge, Iowa 50501 . . . . May 9 - 14
   Crossroads Mall (Combined Units, Rides Only)
Tama, Iowa 52539 . . . . May 18 - 21
   Fire Dept. Carnival (Red Unit)
Centerville, Iowa 52544 . . . . May 23 - 28
   Fire Dept. Carnival (Red Unit)
Belmond, Iowa 50421 . . . . May 30 - June 1
   Jaycees Spring Carnival (Red Unit)
Mason City, Iowa 50401 . . . . June 3 - 5
   State Band Festival (Red Unit)
Fredericksburg, Iowa 50630 . . . . June 7 - 8
   Dairy Days (Red Unit)
Pine Island, Minnesota 55963 . . . . June 10 - 12
   Cheese Festival (Red Unit)
Paynesville, Minnesota 56362 . . . . June 14 - 15
   Town and Country Days (Red Unit)
Janesville Minnesota 56048 . . . . June 17 - 19
   Hay Days (Red Unit)
Mountain Lake, Minnesota 56159 . . . . June 20 - 21
   Pow Wow and Barbeque (Red Unit)
Lake City, Minnesota 55041 . . . . June 24 - 26
   Water Ski Days (Red Unit)
Shell Rock, Iowa 50670 . . . . July 1 - 4
   4th of July Celebration (Red Unit)
St. Charles, Minnesota 55972 . . . . July 6 - 10
   Winona County Fair (Red Unit)
Columbus, Nebraska 68601 . . . . July 13 - 17
   Platte County Fair (Combined Units)
Faribault, Minnesota 55021 . . . . July 19 - 24
   Rice County Fair (Combined Units)
Sioux City, Iowa 51100 . . . . July 26 - 31
   Rivercade (Combined Units)
Anoka, Minnesota 55303 . . . . Aug. 2 - 7
   Anoka County Fair (Combined Units)
Austin, Minnesota 55912 . . . . Aug. 9 - 14
   Mower County Fair (Combined Units)
Owatonna, Minnesota 55060 . . . . Aug. 16 - 21
   Steele County Fair (Combined Units)
Fergus Falls, Minnesota 56537 . . . . Aug. 24 - 27
   Otter Tail County Fair (Combined Units)
Omaha, Nebraska 68131 . . . . Sept. 1 - 5
   Septemberfest (Combined Units)
Mitchell, South Dakota 57301 . . . . Sept. 10 - 18
   Corn Palace (Combined Units)

MERRIAM'S MIDWAY SHOWS, INC.
TEMPE, ARIZONA

1995 ROUTE (BLUE UNIT)

Fort Dodge, Iowa 50501 . . . . May 9 - 14
   Crossroads Mall (Combined Units)
Perry, Iowa 50220 . . . . May 17 - 21
   Chamber of Commerce Spring Carnival (Blue Unit)
Marshalltown, Iowa 50158 . . . . May 24 - 29
   Meadowlane Mall (Blue Unit)
Norfolk, Nebraska 68701 . . . . June 1 - 4
   Sunset Plaza Giant Spring Carnival (Blue Unit)
Blair, Nebraska 68008 . . . . June 8 - 10
   Gateway to the West Celebration (Blue Unit)
North Platte, Nebraska 69101 . . . . June 13 - 19
   Nebraskaland Days (Blue Unit)
Barnesville, Minnesota 56514 . . . . June 22 - 25
   Clay County Fair (Blue Unit)
Bemidji, Minnesota 56601 . . . . June 29 - July 4
   Jaycees Water Carnival (Blue Unit)
Redwood Falls, Minnesota 56283 . . . . July 6 - 9
   Redwood County Fair (Blue Unit)
Columbus, Nebraska 68601 . . . . July 12 - 16
   Platte County Fair (Combined Units)
Faribault, Minnesota 55021 . . . . July 18 - 23
   Rice County Fair (Combined Units)
Sioux City, Iowa 51101 . . . . July 25 - 30
   Rivercade (Combined Units)
Anoka, Minnesota 55303 . . . . Aug. 1 - 6
   Anoka County Fair (Combined Units)
Austin, Minnesota 55912 . . . . Aug. 8 - 13
   Mower County Fair (Combined Units)
Owatonna, Minnesota 55060 . . . . Aug. 15 - 20
   Steele County Fair (Combined Units)
Fergus Falls, Minnesota 56537 . . . . Aug. 23 - 26
   Otter Tail County Fair (Combined Units)
Omaha, Nebraska 68108 . . . . Aug. 31 - Sept. 4
   Septemberfest (Combined Units)
Mitchell, South Dakota 57301 . . . . Sept. 9 - 17
   Corn Palace (Combined Units)

MERRIAM'S MIDWAY SHOWS, INC.
TEMPE, ARIZONA

1995 ROUTE (RED UNIT)

Fort Dodge, Iowa 50501 . . . . May 9 - 14
    Crossroads Mall (Combined Units, Rides Only)
Tama, Iowa 52339 .515-.459-.4822 . . . . May 17 - 20
    Fire Dept. Carnival (Red Unit)
Centerville, Iowa 52544 . . . . May 23 - 29
    Fire Dept. Carnival (Red Unit)
Mason City, Iowa 50401 515-.420-.2017 (evening) June 2 - June 4
    State Band Festival (Red Unit)
Belmond, Iowa 50421 . 515-.444-.4634 . . . . . . June 5 - 7
    Jaycees Spring Carnival (Red Unit)
Pine Island, Minnesota 55963 507-.356-.8255 June 9 - 11
    Cheese Festival (Red Unit)
Fredericksburg, Iowa 50630 319-.237-.5973 . June 13 - 14
    Dairy Days (Red Unit)
Janesville, Minnesota 56048 507-.234-.5499 . June 16 - 18
    Hay Days (Red Unit)
Mountain Lake, Minnesota 56159 507-.427-.3235 June 19 - 20
    Pow Wow and Barbeque (Red Unit)
Lake City, Minnesota 55041 612-.345-.5057 June 23 - 25
    Water Ski Days (Red Unit)
Paynesville, Minnesota 56362 612-.243-.3780 June 27 - 28
    Town and Country Days (Red Unit)
Woodbury, Minnesota 55125 . . . . June 30 - July 4
    Woodbury Days 4th of July Celebration (Red Unit)
St. Charles, Minnesota 55972 507-.932-.6175. July 5 - 9
    Winona County Fair (Red Unit)
Columbus, Nebraska 68601 .402-.562-.6038 . July 12 - 16
.464.3913 Platte County Fair (Combined Units)
Faribault, Minnesota 55021 507-.332-.0912, . July 18 - 23
    Rice County Fair (Combined Units)
Sioux City, Iowa 51101 712-.252-.3364 . . July 25 - 30
    Rivercade (Combined Units)
Anoka, Minnesota 55303 612-.576.9108 . . . Aug. 1 - 6
    Anoka County Fair (Combined Units)
Austin, Minnesota 55912 507-.437-.4747 . . Aug. 8 - 13
    Mower County Fair (Combined Units)
Owatonna, Minnesota 55060 507-.444-.0869 . Aug. 15 - 20
    Steele County Fair (Combined Units)
Fergus Falls, Minnesota 56537 218-.739-.3418 Aug. 23 - 26
    Otter Tail County Fair (Combined Units)
Omaha, Nebraska 68108 . 402-.457-.4662 .Aug. 31 - Sept. 4
    Septemberfest (Combined Units)
Mitchell, South Dakota 57301 605-.995-.6326 Sept. 9 - 17
    Corn Palace (Combined Units)

MERRIAM'S MIDWAY SHOWS, INC.
1949 Our fiftieth annual tour 1998

1998 BLUE UNIT ROUTE

Fort Dodge, Iowa 50501 . . . . May 12 – 17
    Crossroads Mall
Perry, Iowa 50220 . . . . May 20 – 24
    Chamber of Commerce Spring Carnival
Sioux Falls, South Dakota . . . . .May 27 – 31
    Billion Auto Spring Carnival
Norfolk, Nebraska 68701 .June 3 – 7
    Giant Spring Carnival
Blair, Nebraska 68008 . . . . June 11 – 13
    Gateway to the West Celebration
North Platte, Nebraska 69101 . . . . June 16 – 22
    Nebraskaland Days
Cedar Falls, Iowa 50613 . . . . .June 25 – 28
    Sturgis Falls Celebration
Bemidji, Minnesota 56601 . . . . July 1 – 5
    Jaycees Water Carnival
Barnesville, Minnesota 56514 . . . . July 9 – 12
    Clay County Fair
Columbus, Nebraska 68601 . . . . .July 15 – 19
    Platte County Fair (Combined Units)
Sioux City, Iowa 51101 . . . . July 22 – 26
    River-Cade (Combined Units)
Mason City, Iowa 50401 . . . . July 29 – Aug. 2
    North Iowa Fair (Combined Units)
Redwood Falls, Minnesota 56282 . . . . Aug. 6 – 9
    Redwood County Fair (Combined Unit)
Austin, Minnesota 55912 . . . . Aug. 11 – 16
    Mower County Fair (Combined Units)
Owatonna, Minnesota 55060 . . . . Aug. 18 – 23
    Steele County Free Fair (Combined Units)
Fergus Falls, Minnesota 56537 . . . . Aug. 26 – 29
    West Otter Tail County Fair (Combined Units)
Wagner, South Dakota 57380 . . . . Sept. 5 – 7
    Labor Day Celebration (Combined Units)
Mitchell, South Dakota 57301 . . . . Sept. 12 – 20
    Corn Palace (Combined Units)

154

MERRIAM'S MIDWAY SHOWS, INC.
1949 Our fiftieth annual tour 1998

1998 RED UNIT ROUTE

Tama, Iowa 52339 .... May 13 – 16
Fire Dept. Carnival
Centerville, Iowa 52544 .... May 19 – 25
Fire Dept. Carnival
Mason City, Iowa 50401.................... May 29 – 31
State Band Festival
Belmond, Iowa 50421........................ June 1 – 3
Jaycees Spring Carnival
Pine Island, Minnesota 55963 .... June 5 – 7
Cheese Festival
Fredericksburg, Iowa 50630 .... June 9 – 10
Dairy Days
Mountain Lake, Minnesota 56159 .... June 12 – 13
Pow Wow Days
Paynesville, Minnesota 56362................ June 16 –17
Town & Country Days
Janesville, Minnesota 56159 .... June 19 – 21
Hay Days
Lake City, Minnesota 55041 .... June 26 – 28
Water Ski Days
Cannon Falls, Minnesota 55009 .... July 1 – 4
Cannon Valley Fair
St. Charles, Minnesota 55972 .... July 7 – 12
Winona County Fair
Columbus, Nebraska 68601 .... July 15 – 19
Platte County Fair (Combined Units)
Sioux City, Iowa 51101 .... July 22 – 26
River-Cade (Combined Units)
Mason City, Iowa 50401.................... July 29 – Aug. 2
North Iowa Fair (Combined Units)
Redwood Falls, Minnesota 56282 .... Aug. 6 – 9
Redwood County Fair (Combined Unit)
Austin, Minnesota 55912 .... Aug. 11 – 16
Mower County Fair (Combined Units)
Owatonna, Minnesota 55060 .... Aug. 18 – 23
Steele County Free Fair (Combined Units)
Fergus Falls, Minnesota 56537 .... Aug. 26 – 29
West Otter Tail County Fair (Combined Units)
Wagner, South Dakota 57380 .... Sept. 5 – 7
Labor Day Celebration (Combined Units)
Mitchell, South Dakota 57301................. Sept. 12 – 20
Corn Palace (Combined Units)

MERRIAM'S MIDWAY SHOWS, INC.

Continuous family fun since 1949

1999 ANNUAL TOUR 1999

Tama, Iowa 52339 (Red Unit) .... May 12 – 16
  Fire Department Carnival
Fort Dodge, Iowa 50501 (Blue Unit) .... May 11 – 16
  Crossroads Mall
Belmond, Iowa 50421 (Red Unit) .... May 17 – 19
  Jaycees Spring Carnival
Mason City, Iowa 50401 (Red Unit) .... May 21 – 23
  North Iowa Band Festival
Pending (Blue Unit) .... May 19 – 23

Centerville, Iowa 52544 (Red Unit) .... May 26, 31
  Fire Department Carnival
Sioux Falls, South Dakota 57101 (Blue Unit) .... May 27 – June 6
  Billion Auto Spring Carnival
Pine Island, Minnesota 55963 (Red Unit) .... June 4 – 6
  Cheese Festival
Fredericksburg, Iowa 50630 (Red Unit) .... June 8 – 9
  Dairy Days
Waterville, Minnesota 56096 (Red Unit) .... June 11 – 13
  Bullhead Days
Blair, Nebraska 68008 (Blue Unit) .... June 10 – 12
  Gateway to the West Celebration
Paynesville, Minnesota 56362 (Red Unit) .... June 15 – 16
  Town & Country Days
Janesville, Minnesota 56048 (Red Unit) .... June 18 – 20
  Hay Days
North Platte, Nebraska 69101 (Blue Unit) .... June 15 – 21
  Nebraskaland Days
Lake City, Minnesota 55041 (Red Unit) .... June 25 – 27
  Water Ski Days
Cedar Falls, Iowa 50513 (Blue Unit) .... June 24 – 27
  Sturgis Falls Celebration
Cannon Falls, Minnesota 55009 (Red Unit) .... July 1 – 4
  Cannon Valley Fair
Bemidji, Minnesota 56601 (Blue Unit) .... June 30 – July 4
  Jaycees Water Carnival
St. Charles, Minnesota 55972 (Red Unit) .... July 6 – 11
  Winona County Fair
Barnesville, Minnesota 56514 (Blue Unit) .... July 8 – 11
  Clay County Fair
Columbus Nebraska 68601 (Combined Units) .... July 14 – 18
  Platte County Fair
Sioux City, Iowa 51101 (Combined Units) .... July 21 – 25
  River-Cade
Mason City, Iowa 50401 (Red Unit) .... July 28 – August 1
  North Iowa Fair
Madison, Nebraska 68748 (Blue Unit) .... July 28 – August 1
  Madison County Fair and Rodeo
Redwood Falls, Minnesota 56283 (Red Unit) .... August 3 – 8
  Redwood county Fair
Fergus Falls, Minnesota 56537 (Blue Unit) .... August 4 – 7
  Otter Tail county Fair
Austin, Minnesota 55912 (Combined Units) .... August 10 – 15
  Mower County Fair
Owatonna, Minnesota 55060 (Combined Units) .... August 17 – 22
  Steele County Free Fair
Pending (Red Unit) .... August 24 – 29

Sioux Falls, South Dakota 57101 (Blue Unit) .... August 25 – 31
  Billion Auto Fall Carnival
Wagner, South Dakota 57380 (Combined Units) .... September 4 – 6
  Labor Day Celebration
Bentonville, Arkansas 72712 (Combined Units) .... September 14 – 18
  Benton County Fair

Merriam's Midway Shows
Continuous family fun since 1949
2001 NEW MILLENNIUM TOUR 2001

Somerset, Texas 78069 (Red Unit)
   American Legion Chili Cook-off ....March 22-25
Okeene, Oklahoma 73718 (Red Unit)
   Rattlesnake Hunt ....May 3-6
Fort Dodge, Iowa 50501 (Blue Unit)
   Crossroads Mall Spring Carnival.....................May 12-20
Tama, Iowa 52339 (Red Unit)
   Fire Department Carnival ....May 16-19
Centerville, Iowa 52544 (Red Unit)
   Fire Department Carnival ....May 22-28
Davenport, Iowa 52801 (Blue Unit)
   KAABA Shrine Carnival ....May 23-28
LaVista (Omaha), Nebraska 68103 (Blue Unit)
   LaVista Days.....................................May 31-June 3
Mason City, Iowa 50401 (Red Unit)
   North Iowa Band Festival ....June 1-3
Belmond, Iowa 50421 (Red Unit)
   Jaycees Spring Carnival ....June 4-6
Blair, Nebraska 68008 (Blue Unit)
   Gateway to the West Celebration.......................June 7-9
Pine Island, Minnesota 55963 (Red Unit)
   Cheese Festival..June 8-10
Fredericksburg, Iowa 50630 (Red Unit)
   Dairy Days...June 12-13
North Platte, Nebraska 69101 (Blue Unit)
   Nebraskaland Days ....June 12-18
Janesville, Minnesota 56159 (Red Unit)
   Hay Days...June 15-17
Cedar Falls, Iowa 50613 (Blue Unit)
   Sturgis Falls Celebration...............................June 21-24
Lake City, Minnesota 55041 (Red Unit)
   Water Ski Days ....June 22-24
Barnesville, Minnesota 56514 (Blue Unit)
   Clay County Fair..June 28-July 1
Cannon Falls, Minnesota 55009 (Red Unit)
   Cannon Valley Fair....................................June 30-July 4
Bemidji, Minnesota 56601 (Blue Unit)
   Jaycees Water Carnival ....July 4-8
St. Charles, Minnesota 55972 (Red Unit)
   Winona County Fair...July 5-8
Columbus, Nebraska 68601 (Combined Units)
   Platte County Fair ....July 11-15
Sioux City, Iowa 51101 (Combined Units)
   River-Cade...July 17-22
Huron, South Dakota 57350 (Combined Units)
   South Dakota State Fair....................July 28-August 5
Austin, Minnesota 55912 (Combined Units)
   Mower County Fair ....August 7-12
Owatonna, Minnesota 55060 (Combined Units)
   Steele County Free Fair.............................August 14-19
Lisbon, North Dakota 58054 (Combined Units)
   Ransom County Fair ....August 22-26
Wagner, South Dakota 57380 (Combined Units)
   Labor Day Celebration...........................September 1-3
Spencer, Iowa 51301 (Combined Units)
   Clay County Fair ....September 8-16

60th Anniversary World Tour

Merriam's Midway Shows
2009 -- Route -- 2009

May 13 – 16 . . . . Tama, Iowa 52339
   (Todd's Unit) Fire Department Carnival
May 22 – 25 . . . . Mason City, Iowa 50401
   (Todd's Unit) North Iowa Band Festival
May 28 – 31 . . . . .Waterloo, Iowa 50701
   (Both Units) My Waterloo Days
June 4 – 7 . . . . .Omaha, Nebraska 69105
   (Todd's Unit) Shopping Center Pending
June 3 – 6 . . . . Fort Dodge, Iowa 50501
   (Dale's Unit) Crossroads Mall
June 9 – 10 . . . . Fredericksburg, Iowa 50630
   (Dale's Unit) Dairy Day
June 11 - 13 . . . . Blair, Nebraska 68008
   (Todd's Unit) Gateway to the West
June 12 - 14. . . . . Pine Island, Minnesota 55963
   (Dale's Unit) Cheese Festival
June 17 - 22 . . . . Winona, Minnesota 55987
   (Both Units) Steamboat Days
June 25 –28 . . . . Cedar Falls, Iowa 50613
   (Todd's Unit) Sturgis Falls Days
June 26 – 28 . . . . Lake City, Minnesota 55041
   (Dale's Unit) Water Ski Days
July 1 - 5 . . . . .Bemidji, Minnesota 56601
   (Todd's Unit) Water Carnival
July 3 – 5 . . . . Albert Lea, Minnesota 56007
   (Dale's Unit) 4th of July Celebration
July 8 - 12 . . . . Columbus, Nebraska 68601
   (Both Units) Platte County Fair
July 15 - 19 . . . . Sioux City, Iowa 51101
   (Both Units) River-Cade
July 22 – 26 . . . . Jordan, Minnesota 55352
   (Todd's Unit) Scott County Fair
July 24 – 26 . . . . Hayfield, Minnesota 55940
   (Dale's Unit) Hey Days
July 30 – Aug. 2 . . Redwood Falls, Minnesota 56283
   (Todd's Unit) Redwood County Fair
July 31 – Aug. 2 . . . . . Claremont, Minnesota 55924
   (Dale's Unit) Hog Fest
Aug. 4 – 9 . . . . Albert Lea, Minnesota 56007
   (Both Units) Freeborn County Fair
Aug. 11 – 16 . . . . Austin, Minnesota 55912
   (Both Units) Mower County Fair
Aug. 18 – 23 . . . . Owatonna, Minnesota 55060
   (Both Units) Steele County Free Fair
Aug. 26 – 30 . . . . Lisbon, North Dakota 58054
   (Dale's Unit) Ransom County Fair
Sept. 5 – 7 . . . . Wagner, South Dakota 57380
   (Dale's Unit) Labor Day Celebration
Sept. 12 – 20 . . . . Spencer, Iowa 51301
   (Both Units) Clay County Fair

Alva C. Merriam
1949 -- 1973

Dale W. Merriam
1974 – 2002

Todd D. Merriam
2003 –

Favorite Recipes
Of the
Merriam Family

Alicia Merriam

Over the years I've spun the candy and dipped the dogs, but my favorite recipes I've saved for my friends.

Here are a few for you to enjoy.

Alicia Merriam

Todd's Margaritas

(Margaret Atkins' recipe. Todd bought it at an OABA
Jamboree for "Big bucks")

12 oz frozen limeade, thawed

12 oz tequila (Jose' Quaver)

12 oz 7-Up

12 oz (Miller Lite) beer

Pour in punch bowl or pitcher and add ice. Rim glassed with
lime juice then salt in shallow dish. Garnish glasses with one
half thin lime slice.

*Many of our fair board members have enjoyed these at Show Parties
held during their fair.*

RECIPES

* Pine Island (ordering Band Uniform)
B-B-Q recipe for Cheese Festival Stand in main streets (started to buy his Band Uniforms)

B-B-Q

2 lbs. ground beef (Had a wonderful meat market next door)
1 ½ cup chopped onions
4 T. fat (if using less fatty brand)
1 t. salt
¼ t. pepper
2 cans chicken gumbo soup
½ can water (rinse soup can(
2 T. catsup
2 T Worcestershire sauce
2 cups finely chopped celery

Brown meat, onion, celery in fat, add all other ingredients and simmer about 20 minutes. (Gals used to bring large batches in roasters to stand.)

*Serve on hamb. Bund - $1.00 each.

Recipe came from Kay Starz Banitt, her mom Bernise, one of the great P. I. cooks!

No Bull Ranch Slaw
A great tasting Arizona treat

½ head green cabbage, sliced thin and chopped
2 green onions, chopped
1 pkg. (Nisson) Top Ramen Oriental Noodle Soup (chicken flavor)
Toasted: 2 T sliced almonds, 2T sesame seeds, & the broken up noodles

Dressing: Combine in jar 2T sugar, ½ cup olive oil, ¾ t salt, ½ t cracked pepper, 3T red wine vinegar (Regina is best), 1pkg Top Ramen Flavoring (cones with the noodles). Toss salad with dressing at the last minute.

Special Touch: cooked chicken breast (shredded), Mandarin oranges (drained).

Iowa Corn Dip
(What Else?)

10 oz (2 ½ Monterey jack / cheddar cheese – shredded)
15 oz. (1 ½ cups) corn (drained) or cut fresh cooked corn off the cob
4 oz. can diced green chilies - drained
½ c Hellmann's (Best Foods – west of the Rockies) mayonnaise
½ c sour cream
3 – 4 green onions, diced
1-2 jalapeños, diced

Mix all together.

Serve with tortilla chips.

Chicken Enchiladas
Even my Hubby, Dale, who doesn't like chicken, loves this recipe!

4 whole chicken breasts
2 (10 ¾ oz.) cans cream of chicken soup
2 (4 oz.) cans whole green chilies
½ teaspoon leaf oregano
¼ teaspoon each, ground cumin, ground sage, & chili powder
2 gloves garlic, pressed
1 pound longhorn cheese, grated (Kraft is good)
¼ pound jack cheese, grated
2 large onions, diced coarsely
1 package (12) corn tortillas
Cooking oil

Salt (easy) and pepper chicken. Enclose tightly in a foil. Bake at 350 degrees about 1 hour. Cool and de-bone.

Chalupas
Served at many Fiesta Bowl tailgates

3 pound pork loin or butt (boneless)
2 garlic cloves, minced
1 tsp oregano
1 Tbs plus 1 tsp ground cumin
1 tsp salt
1 can (14.5 oz.) Hunts diced tomatoes
2 cans (14.5) of chicken broth
1 onion chopped
2 cans (7 oz.) diced green chilies
1 pound dry pinto beans, rinsed
¼ tsp crushed red pepper

Garnish: grated cheese, chopped onions, sour scream, avocado sauce, diced tomatoes, shredded lettuce, salsa, black olives, chips.

Trim excess fat off pork. Place all of the ingredients into a large crock pot. Cover and cook on high for about 7 hours. Break up meat into shredded pieces, cook the juice down a bit and taste for seasoning. Serve over a crisp corn tostada or tortilla chips, and serve with the desired condiments. Encouraging the guests to try all the toppings makes the dish fun and special.

Six Layer Brownie Bars

A big hit with our carnival crew and high dollar seller at the Jamboree.

½ cup (1 stick) butter, melted
1 box Ghirardelli Double Chocolate Brownie mix
1 cup shredded coconut
2 cups semi-sweet chocolate chips
1 cup chopped pecas
1 ¼ cup (14 oz. can) sweetened condensed milk "Eagle Brand"

Preheat oven to 350 degrees. Coat bottom of 13 x 9 x 2 –inch pan with parchment paper and Pam. Sprinkle brownie mix with melted butter in bowl and pour and press in bottom of prepared pan. Top with coconut, chocolate chips and pecans. Drizzle with sweetened condensed milk. Bake 30-35 minutes or until edges are bubbly. Cool thoroughly before cutting. Refrigerate, then cut again and refrigerate again. Best eaten cold. Makes 24 2-inch bars.

Lemon Bars

Another Todd favorite. . . "Mom, where are you
going to make those lemon bars?"

2 cups flour
1 cup butter, soft
½ cup powdered sugar

Mix with pastry blender and press in 9x13 pan (You're on the road, use an aluminum throw away). Line pan with parchment paper, and spray with Pam. Bake 20 minutes at 350 degrees.

4 eggs
2 cups sugar (white)
1/3 cup lemon juice, plus lemon zest (1 tsp) to your taste
½ tsp baking powder
Pinch of salt

Mix with beater and pour into hot crust.

Bake 25 minutes at 350 degrees. Cool. Dust with powdered sugar. Refrigerate and cut into bars.

Lightning Source UK Ltd.
Milton Keynes UK
UKHW011018080320
359965UK00001B/76

9 781728 34796